The Complete BONSAI Handbook

The Complete BONSAI Handbook

Darlene Dunton

 STEIN AND DAY/*Publishers*/Briarcliff Manor, N.Y.

First published in 1979
Copyright © 1979 by Darlene Dunton
All rights reserved.
Designed by Ed Kaplin
Printed in the United States of America
Stein and Day/*Publishers*/Scarborough House,
Briarcliff Manor, N.Y. 10510

Library of Congress Cataloging in Publication Data

Dunton, Darlene.
   The complete bonsai handbook.

   Includes index.
   1. Bonsai.   I. Title.
SB433.5.D86   635.9'77   78-6527
ISBN 0-8128-2510-1
ISBN 0-8128-6008-X pbk.

To my wonderful parents, Raymond and Cleo Stephens,
with all my love

ACKNOWLEDGMENTS

Cleo Stephens, the photo-journalist, has been my inspiration; without her help this book would not have come into being.

So many people have been generous with their help and advice. My deepest gratitude to Ann Pipe, friend and mentor—to Sandra Christophel—to Mr. and Mrs. Wagner of the House of Bonsai, Naples, Florida—to Edward Zenz—to Jean Waterhout—to Ken Lutrell—to Joel Gold, for the use of his fine photographs and bonsai skill—to Melanie and Paula, for tiptoeing when Mother was upstairs typing—and most of all to my husband, Dale, who shares his knowledge and talent without ceasing.

Contents

Introduction

The great tree stands on the slope of a hill, spreading wide, gracious arms in mute benediction. Birds nest here, breezes play through the leaves, wild things pause in its cool shelter, lovers dream beneath this majestic being. It is huge, quiet, strong, dear to my heart, the object of my admiration. Each season passing is accepted as it comes, leaving the tree more beautiful, more filled with dignity. I know it is many times older then the span of my life and may very well shelter my children after me. I love it and I cannot have it—must move here and there through life's needs. I may not stay near to draw strength and inspiration.

But can I not build a model, a living, growing replica? All humankind appreciates Nature and must hold it in some way. Bonsai came into being in reply to this need.

What more can be said of bonsai? The market is well supplied with excellent books dealing with the subject—some complicated and technical for the advanced enthusiast, others for the newest beginners. There's even an in-between phase represented: lovely books filled with fine color pictures of famous bonsai for us to study and enjoy.

This book deals with aspects heretofore ignored or neglected: indoor cultivation of single trees, groves, and landscapes, using both natural and artificial light; the collection and training of native North American trees and plants; improvement of poorly trained or substandard trees; and the design and making of containers. None of the basic processes is neglected. The beginner will not find it confusing, and the advanced grower will discover some new ideas and methods.

Perhaps the most useful of these techniques are those that help assure the life and health of your trees during your absence. You'll be shown how to automate care of the trees for a month or more, making possible a worry-free vacation or allowing for a long workday and other circumstances when it is impossible to be on hand for watering at just the right time.

Some of the methods of the bonsai master have been secret until recently;

they will be described and illustrated. Bonsai can be very intricate or beautifully simple. You can delve into it to the degree that suits you and find deep satisfaction in a pastime that involves a constant process of improving and developing, becoming ever more absorbing.

1–1 *Komono*: Some of the small-leafed citrus are interesting prospects; Narco orange, 7 inches.

1. Standards to Follow or Ignore

There is good reason to phrase this chapter title as it is here, because while it is a great help to know the basic, established criteria of beauty and value for traditional bonsai, there are times when a stunning tree conforms to none of the usual specifications.

It's important to know accepted methods of design and style that can give you the confidence to go eventually beyond the book to higher appreciation and personal satisfaction. No great writer, composer, or painter became great by blindly following rules dictated by others. Each set his or her own path and struck sympathetic chords in the hearts of an appreciative audience.

JUDGING BONSAI

The standards we offer here are those that are recognized worldwide. If you decide to depart from them after you read this book, it will be through informed choice, not ignorance. That's the difference between knowledge and wisdom.

INITIAL IMPACT OF THE ENTIRE COMPOSITION

The first impression one receives of the overall creation is naturally of principal importance.

Training and Design

The tree should be neatly pruned with no ragged, unkempt stubs and no awkward, ill-planned wiring. All wiring should be neat and well placed and must not bite into the branches. The tree must sit at the best angle in the pot, neither too high, too low, too much to one side or the other, nor precisely in the middle.

Roots

The roots should grasp the ground firmly and deploy with a fair degree of evenness.

Trunk

The surface of the trunk should look like that of an old, established tree with bark which is typical of its species. A shapely, well-tapered trunk is essential.

Branches

There must be good balance in the angle and positioning of the branches, with thoughtfully placed unoccupied areas, "for the birds and butterflies," as one master grower liked to put it. The more twigginess the better.

Scale

The leaves or needles should be small enough to look as if they belonged on a tree of this size. This also applies to flowers and fruits.

General Health

A dying or struggling tree is not a pleasing sight and defeats the original purpose of bonsai. Glowing good health is always beautiful and is an important criterion. This is one rule that should not be ignored. See the *Driftwood* entry in the style classification section, below. Even here the foliage must look healthy.

Ground Cover or Soil Surface

Careless maintenance shows up here. If the moss or other groundcover is weedy, thin, or in poor condition, if the soil surface is littered with debris, the tree will not look its best.

Relationship of Tree to Container and Accessories

Even though it's far down on this list, the choice of a container and base or accessories is crucial to the overall appearance.

Grooming

It's easy to overlook a few spiderwebs, an empty insect shell, dead leaves, mineral deposits on the soil surface or pot, a little dust or smudges on the pot. But when you think of the bonsai as a whole you realize that any untidiness distracts one's attention and detracts from the intended image of beauty and order.

SIZE CLASSIFICATIONS

Measurements in the text are from the ground up, not including the pot.

(Measurements in the photo captions include the pot.) The four smaller categories are as follows:

Keshitsubu
(Pea size) Up to 3 inches (7.6 cm). The tiniest and most difficult of all. Not commonly seen.

Mamé (Mah-máy)
(Baby) Between 3 and 6 inches (7.6–15 cm). A charming size, but not as useful or ostentatious as larger sizes (See color plates).

Komono
(Fig. 1–1) Between 6 and 9 inches (15–20 cm). (See also color plates.)

Katade-Mochi
(Figs. 1–2, 3) About 9 to 18 inches (20.3–46 cm). (See also color plates.)

All the above are easy to move with one hand and are often called "One-Hand" or "Fingertip" bonsai. The larger sizes range from "Two-Hand" to "One-Man," "Two-Man," and even "Four-man," meaning it would take this much strength to move them. The two sizes listed below fall into the larger categories:

Chumono
(Fig. 1-4) About 18 to 36 inches (46–91 cm).

Onomo
Over 36 inches (91 cm).

STYLE CLASSIFICATIONS

Formal Upright (Chokkan)
(Figs. 1–5, 6) Single tree with straight trunk tapering from ground to tip. The branches usually radiate from the trunk in such a way that the view from the top (looking down on the tree) shows fairly even, balanced branching on all sides.

From the front, about two-thirds of the total trunk length should show, either through the branches at intervals or from the ground to the first branch. (Glimpses of the trunk always should show among the branches.)

The branch arrangement is classic: Starting at the ground, the first branch should be the thickest and longest, pointing to one side or very slightly toward the front. The second is at the opposite side, higher than the first, and the third is toward the back, higher than the second. Back branches are very important

1–2 *Katade-Mochi*: Abelia, 12 inches. *(Ann Pipe collection. Cleo Stephens, photo)*

1–3 Katade Muchi: Pyracantha, 10 inches. *(Ann Pipe collection. Cleo Stephens, photo)*

4

1-4 *Chumono:* A very old imported ginkgo, 30 inches *(Ann Pipe collection. Cleo Stephens, photo)* 1-5 Formal Upright: A fine old Yew *(Taxus capitata),* 27 inches *(Ann Pipe collection. Cleo Stephens, photo)* 1-6 Formal Upright: Wild shadblow *(Amalanchier canadensis),* 18 inches. Another of our native trees that makes good bonsai. *(Dunton collection)*

for without them to give it a third dimension the tree will have a fish-bone look. The apex or tip of the tree should tilt slightly toward the front for a more pleasing appearance and to indicate the front.

This basic framework of main branches is filled in with secondary branches. The whole plan follows the "rule of one-third": The lowest branch is roughly one-third of the way up the trunk with the others positioned above in a natural, random pattern.

Informal Upright (Moyogi), or Slanting (Shakan)

(Figs. 1–7, 8) The same planning suggestions apply here, but the trunk slants and sometimes has a slight curve. (See also color plates.)

Cascade (Kengai)

(Fig. 1–9) The main trunk rises fairly straight up from the ground, starting at a point near the edge of the tall, narrow pot. It forms a curve to cascade over the opposite edge and down to below the lip of the pot. The tip of such a tree may reach below the base of the pot when it is grown and shown on a tall, slender pedestal. Such trees are often grown with more than one trunk.

Although the branches curve downward, each tip should show vitality by pointing upward. Branches wired with their tips pointing downward don't thrive and often die.

If a cascade seems to be losing its vigor it can be grown for a time on its side. This technique usually restores vitality to the downward growing branches. (See also color plates.)

Semicascade (Han-Kengai)

This is like the cascade but with modifications. The curve is not as precipitous nor as deep; there may be more bulk to the apex area (see fig. 5–4).

The five styles above are the main classifications but there are many others, some of which are variations on these.

Broom

The American elm tends naturally to this style—a single straight trunk and a crown with many tiny twigs radiating out into a broom-like shape. The style is used most often for Zelkova, the Japanese greybark elm (see figs. 4–11,12).

Literati

A striking style with a long, slender trunk that may be straight, slanting, or slightly curved. Branches appear only at the upper third of the tree. The apex should occur at some point over the base of the tree for balance.

1-7 Informal Upright: Florida Buttonwood, 20 inches. (*Wagner collection*) 1-8 Detail showing weathered roots.

1-9 Cascade: An interesting way to display a 2½-inch juniper cascade. (*Joel Gold Collection. Cleo Stephens, photo*)

7

1-10 Grove: Italian Cypress, 22 inches, a good plant for groves. *(Wagner collection)*
1-11 Grove: Pistachio, 18 inches. The accessory is a very old Chinese toy. *(Ann Pipe collection. Cleo Stephens, photo)*

Driftwood (Jin)

Some of the trunk or branches have died and been made into bare driftwood. This can look very dramatic, but the surviving growth should not appear sickly (see fig. 3–2).

Windswept

(See figs. 1–9, 5–8) A tree grown in this style looks as if it has always lived on a windswept crag. The trunk and all the branches are swept in one direction. The style is more easily maintained if it is carefully oriented to the prevailing winds.

Exposed Root

The tree stands stilt-like upon exposed roots (see fig. 2–16).

Rock Planting

The tree can be planted on a flat rock, in the crevice of a rock, or on a tall, craggy rock in a pocket of soil (see fig. 11–13).

Root-over-Rock

(See fig. 7–4) This is a variation of the rock planting arrangement above. Roots of the tree clasp the rock and then grow into the soil.

Raft

All the trees in a raft arrangement are connected. This is accomplished by laying a tree on its side and training the branches as individual trees (see fig. 5–9).

Grove

A group of trees planted in a large shallow tray as a natural grove. In silhouette most groves or clumps or two- and three-tree plantings tend to blend so they appear to be a single tree. Groves are most effective if designed in this way (see figs. 1–10, 11; 18–9).

Saikei

The grove is carried several steps further in this style, which employs trees, mosses, rocks, and tiny shrubs. Sometimes a stream or waterfall is suggested by the use of sand. In-scale statues of people, boats, animals, and the like may be used, but this is seldom done (see figs. 7–1—3).

Cloud or Umbrella

This style, with a single fairly straight trunk and a copious umbrella of foliage on all sides, is lovely for almost any tree, but especially for the multiflora rose. It conforms to the natural growth pattern of many of the *Ficus* species (see fig. 6–2).

On all but the cloud style, the lightning-struck, jin, or driftwood effects can be applied at the apex, sub-apex, or trunk, or to one or more branches, without changing the style designation.

There are endless variations of these styles, and some confusion begins to develop when it is seen that some descriptions overlap one another. The only time that style classifications are really important is at a competition. Then categories must be established to facilitate the awarding of prizes. At such times the organization conducting the event can elect a classification committee. The committee and all competitors must have copies of the specifications, and all concerned must be willing to accept the rulings without complaint. It's easy to see why the Japanese haven't made a habit of judging their bonsai shows.

1–12 A tiny privet (*Ligustrum sp.*) *(Joel Gold collection. Cleo Stephens, photo)*

1–13 Unidentified. *(Yucca sp.?) (Joel Gold collection. Cleo Stephens, photo)*

2. Obtaining Plants

UNDERSTANDING PLANT NAMES

"*Eleagnus augusti* what? The scientific names of plants may sound (depending upon whose ears they fall) pretentious, preposterous, phony, or altogether fascinating with the pure, unsullied beauty of perfect order.

Before the Swedish botanist Linnaeus developed the binomial system of naming plants, utter chaos reigned in the world of plant nomenclature. A firebush could be anything from an *amaranthus* to a *pyracantha*, a pepper could be *capsicum* or *solanum*. All are very different plants, though who could define and specify the differences?

The binomial (*bi*-two, *nomen*-name) naming of plants is actually like our system of using two personal names: Dunton is a family name; Darlene identifies a specific member of the family. In the same way *ilex* is the family name for holly. *Nudifolia* is a descriptive name which identifies the plant more specifically. So what is *Ilex nudifolia*? *Ilex,* holly; *nudi*—you guessed it—naked or nude; *folia*—just what it sounds like—foliage. Holly with naked stems, deciduous holly! Why go to all this trouble? Latin is the only universal language. It is used throughout the world to describe plants and animals because it doesn't change, it's very old, and scientists of all lands can use the same uncorrupted language.

But just because virtually every living thing has been neatly labeled doesn't mean there'll be no changes. One of the *Sheffeleras* has recently been officially designated as belonging to another family—I forget which one; it took me long enough to learn *Sheffelera*—but basically the names are stable. You can tell your friend on the other side of the world about your *Acer buergerianum* and he will understand you're referring to your trident maple, be he French or Indonesian.

One convincing argument for learning and depending upon Latin plant names is this: If you ordered "Fire Bush" you could get *Pyracantha,*

11

Amaranthus, Euonymous (any one of several dozen varieties), *Kochia*—the list could go on indefinitely. The common name for one plant in any given locality may be completely different only a few miles away. In Europe, linden, *Tillia* family, a deciduous shade tree, is called lime. Here, when we say lime we are talking about a tropical citrus tree which has green lemon-like fruits. So you see the problem of using common names.

The family name and species name may be followed by several other words describing plant color, habit, leaf size, floriferousness, origin, or even the Latinized name of its discoverer. If the last name has quotation marks and is capitalized (ordinarily only the family name is capitalized), it is a special name given to a plant bred by botanists: *Ulmus* (elm) *parvifolia* (small-leaved) "Quickshade" is a specially developed shade tree and "Quickshade" is literally a brand name.

It's useful and gratifying to learn some of these terms. Let's say we are looking for a tall, narrow evergreen plant for a landscape. Should we buy *Juniperous excelsia* (upright) *stricta* (narrow), or *J. procumbens* (procumbent, or lying down) *nana* (dwarf)? You will notice that many of them contain recognizable word-roots: For example, *roseaflora* (rose-like flower), *jasminoides* (like a jasmine). Isn't it more satisfying to know that the tree in the hedgerow on your uncle's farm is not just a wahoo tree, but *Euonymous alata* (winged or corky bark) *atropurpureus* (purple, sometimes dark red)?

The catalogue listings of some of the most desirable bonsai species often use Latin descriptive names. To avoid disappointment, learn a few basic terms or look them up when in doubt. Then if, for instance, you are hesitating between *Ficus* (fig) *macrofolia* (large leaves) and *F. microfolia* (small or very small leaves), you'll make the right choice. Here's a Latin-English plant dictionary that will help you.

abbreviatus——short
acuminatus——long tapering point
acutifolius——with sharp leaves
adpressus——pressed together, pressed against
adscendens——going up
aerius——of the air, as air-roots
affinis——related, with an affinity
africanus——from Africa
alatus——winged
albescens——pale, whitish
albidus, albus——white
albiflorus——with white flowers
alpinus——of the alpines, mountains
alternus——alternating, usually meaning not directly opposite
altus——altitude, tall

amabilis——pretty

amphibius——adaptable either to land or water

angulosus——angled, turning every which way

angustifolius——with narrow leaves (seldom used, more often the term is *nerifolius*)

aquaticus——of the water, water-loving

arborescens——growing like a tree, woody like a tree

arenatius——found in sandy places

argenteus, argentus——silvery

aristatus——bearded

arrectus——straight up, erect

ascendens——going up, ascending

asiaticus, asiatus——from Asia

atlanticus——Atlantic

atropurpureus, atropurpurea——purple, sometimes dark red

atrosanguineus——dark blood-red

atroviolaceus——dark violet

atrovirens——dark green

augustus——imposing, important in size or appearance

aurantiacus——orange-red

aureus——golden

azureus——light blue, azure

babylonicus——Babylonian, from Babylon

balticus——from the Baltic

bengalinis——from Bengal

biennis——biennial

biflorus——two-flowered

bifolius——two-leaved

brefolius——with short leaves

brevis——short

brevisimus——very short

brilliantisimus——brilliant

brittanicus——from Britain

brunneus——brown

bulgarius——Bulgarian

buxifolius——with leaves like a boxwood, box-leaved

calamifolius——with reed-like leaves

californicus——from California

campestris——found in fields

candelabrum——having the form of a candelabra

candicans——white, or frosty looking

catitatus——headed

carneus——flesh-colored

cerefolius——with waxy leaves
coccineus——bright red
coloratus——colored
columnaris——having the form of a column
concolor——similar coloring
conglomeratus——all close together
contortus——twisted, contorted
cordatus——heart-shaped
cornutus, cornuta——horned
crassifolius——with thick leaves
crenatus——serrated
cuspidatus——sharp tooth or hard point
deformis——deformed
deliciosus, deliciosa——delicious
dendroideus——like a tree
densatus——dense
densifolius——with dense leaves
densiflorus——with dense flowers
dentatus——toothed, a series of points
dipterus——two-winged
discolor——of two or several colors
dissectus——deeply cut leaves, as in fern-leaved maple
divaricatus——spreading
domesticus——domesticated
edulis——can be eaten
elatus, elata——tall
elegans——elegant, graceful
elongatus——long
erectus——upright
excelsius, excelsus——tall
exoticus, exotica——from another country
fastigiatus——having nearly vertical, close-together branches
ferox——fierce, thorny
flaccidus——soft, limp
flammeus——flame-colored
flexilis——bendable, flexible
florepleno——with double flowers
floribundus——with many flowers
foetidus——bad-smelling, having a fetid odor
fragrans——sweet-smelling, fragrant
fragrantissimus——very sweet-smelling
frutescens——bushy, shrubby, twiggy
gallicus——from Gaul (France), may also pertain to a rooster

giganticus——large, gigantic

glaucus——with a frost-like bloom, as on a grape

gloriosus, gloriosa——great, superb

gracilis——slender, graceful, lissome

grandifolius——with large leaves

gutatus——freckled

haemanthus——bright red flowers

humilis——dwarf, low

ilicifolius——holly-like leaves

japonicus——from Japan

lancifolius——with lance-like leaves

latifolius——with broad leaves

leptolepis——with thin scales

leptophyllus——with thin leaves

leucodermis——with white skin

lobularis——lobed

luteus——yellow

macranthus——with large flowers

macro——big, long, large

maximus——the largest

medius——medium

megalophyllus——with very large leaves

microphyllus——with very small leaves

minimus——very small

mollis——hairy, fuzzy

myriophyllus——with many leaves

nanus, nana——dwarf, small

nerifolius, nerifolia——with narrow leaves

niger——black

nodulosa——with small nodes

nudifolia——deciduous, naked of leaves

oblongatus——oblong, oval

officinalis——medicinal

parviflorus——with small flowers

parvifolia——with small leaves

patens——spreading

pinous——pine-like

podocarpus——with stalked fruits

polydactylus——with many fingers

porphyreus——purple

praecox——very early

procumbens——procumbent, lying down

pumilus——dwarf, small

pygmaeus——pygmy
pyramidalis——pyramidal
repens——creeping, low
reticulatus——with a netted pattern
robustus——strong, robust
roseaflorus——with rose-like flowers
rotundifolius——with round leaves
scandens——climbing
semperflorens——everblooming
sempervirens——always green
serpens——creeping
serpyllifolius——with thyme-like leaves
serratus——with a saw-tooth edge
stolenifera——with runners that root and send up another plant
strictus——erect
sylvaticus——of the forest
tenuifolius——with slender leaves
tomentosus——very wooly
tridens——with three teeth or points
variegatus——variegated
verrucosus——warty
virens——green
virginianus——of Virginia, first defined in Virginia
viridis——green
vulgaris——common, vulgar, ordinary
xanthinus——yellow
zonalis——banded

MAIL ORDER PLANTS AND SEEDS

Sometimes the only way to obtain a species you want is to order the plant from a mail-order nursery. This can be very satisfactory and is certainly easier than collecting your own, but you should have some realistic idea of what to expect.

Most of the material offered by mail is small, and the trunks are often of matchstick size (figs. 2–1, 2). For deciduous trees and shrubs this is not a serious drawback, since this type develops quickly in just a few years. You can consider such a plant your own creation because you nursed it from infancy.

Pay close attention to size descriptions in the promotional literature. A one-dollar seedling in a 2-inch (5 cm) pot cannot be expected to be more than a tiny switch. A plant from a gallon (3.7 liter) container can often be shaped immediately into a respectable starter-bonsai, and can soon be a valued addition to your display benches.

2–1 A *Larix leptolepsis* seeding in a 2-inch pot. For $1.50–$3.00 you can expect something like this. In 3 to 5 years a promising specimen can be developed. 2–2 This tiny flowering cherry is blooming three weeks after it arrives in the mail!

Beginning with seed is an enjoyable and rewarding method because you control size and growth-pattern completely. This is one of the best ways to start *mamé* material, and is an inexpensive source for groves. Since some tree seeds need to be scarified (nicked, cut, or sandpapered through the hull) or stratified (left for a time in a cool, moist atmosphere), read the seed package instructions carefully.

Experienced growers usually prefer to ignore catalogues that don't give Latin names. These companies sometimes supply inferior stock in precarious health; some deliberately mislead you with wild promises. Catalogues that provide special varietal names, i.e., *Buxus microphylla* "Kingsville" (a superior type of boxwood for bonsai) or *Juniperus chinensis* "Robusta Green" (a fine-textured Chinese Juniper) usually have something better than ordinary and are trying to tell you about it.

Examine farm and garden catalogues for "liners" (one- to three-year old seedlings) or hedging plants. Some of our treasured hedge maple (*Acer ginella*), Chinese elm (*Ulmus parvifolia*), and wild plum (*Prunus sp.*) were ordered from garden catalogues. (See the source list in the final chapter.)

To buy imported or mature bonsai, ask for snapshots of the very tree offered for sale, with views of both sides, front, back, and top. If the tree is worth the price being asked the seller will be glad to supply pictures, and you may be spared great and expensive disappointment!

COLLECTING NATURALLY DWARFED TREES AND SHRUBS

Before setting out on a safari to the woods, pastures, and roadsides, investigate your own lawn and flowerbeds for seedlings of elm, maple, holly, privet, mulberry, hackberry, boxwood, and any other tree or shrub that could be eligible for training. Old ivy and Virginia creeper stumps, carefully lifted, shaped, and trained, can make beautiful specimens.

COLLECTING FROM THE WILD

Getting permission from property owners is the first consideration. Make sure you know property boundaries, close all gates behind you, fill holes made when digging, and leave not a trace of disturbance. Write your state conservation office for a list of protected species, and observe all restrictions.

The middle of a deep woods is fun to explore but seldom can offer the kind of plant you seek. Look in pastures and around the graze. Fence-rows present good possibilities, as do country roadsides and the shores of ponds (figs. 2–3, 4). Rocky hillsides and cliffs are another matter; the lovely trees there may be impossible to remove because of the excessively long roots that follow cracks in the rocks. Always check this possibility before you do much serious digging. If you are a determined soul, be prepared to salvage many long, coarse roots, to be pruned back gradually over the years to come (figs. 2–5, 6).

EQUIPMENT

Your collecting kit should include a small, well-sharpened garden spade, a large shovel, a hand trowel, an axe, two crowbars (if the terrain is rocky), large pruners, burlap or heavy plastic to wrap soil-balls, rope to secure the wrapping material, and a spray-can of Wilt-proof or a similar anti-transpirant product. Also include a handful of small plastic bags in which to collect seeds, small plants, or moss, and, if there is any likelihood of digging up a heavy tree, a large dragging-canvas.

Wear comfortable boots and sturdy slacks. Bring work gloves and be prepared for stick-tights, snakes, sunburn, curious or aggressive livestock, hornets (they nest around fruit trees), and a good hike. Don't be disappointed if you find nothing worth collecting; there's always another day, and it's a great adventure to walk over God's creation and be close to it for a time.

2–3 Red mangrove, 18 inches. Note oysters on roots. 2–4 Red mangrove, 18 inches. This one had few roots below the soil, and has apparently been moved successfully but time will tell. Red mangrove is protected in Florida. This one was taken because it was in the path of fishing boats which often ran it over.

2–5 A very old 22-inch maple collected by John Lowrance. Long internodes and large leaves will be reduced by leaf-pruning. 2–6 The trunk shows a great deal of character.

TO DIG A TREE WITH AN UNDISTURBED SOIL BALL

It's usually best to collect plants during their dormant season, but if you've any doubt about how well it will travel, prune any expendable top growth and apply anti-transpirant to any foliage.

Don't thrust the spade under the plant and lift unless it's a small plant and the ground is soft and moist. The better way is to dig a trench around the specimen, exploring with fingers and trowel to see how well the root ball is being circled. When the trench reaches below the main bulk of the roots, begin to cut and dig under the ball, severing the taproot only if absolutely necessary. Using the shovel, reach under and rock the ball to one side enough to slip a burlap or strong plastic sheet partially under, tilt it to the other side and pull the wrapping through, then wrap the ball and tie it firmly. Lift your prize out of the ground, refill the hole using surrounding soil, and level the area.

When circumstances permit, a safer but more drawn-out method is root cutting. The top of the plant is partially reduced and a sharp shovel is thrust vertically into the ground at several points around the plant, cutting one-third to one-half of the roots the first season, preferably in early spring, and one-third to one-half the second season. The plant is lifted and moved during the second or third operation. This gives it time to form roots closer to the trunk before the actual transplanting (figs. 2–7, 8).

Never jostle the plant and don't lift it by the trunk; that trunk is not a handle, it's your tree's body and any pulling could separate enough roots from the trunk to kill it. Another reason is that bark often shows blemishes months, even years, after being roughly handled. Avoid pressing or gripping any bonsai trunk whenever you work with it.

Even a dormant tree gives off some moisture, so keep it out of drying winds and cover the roots well. Even if you've used anti-transpirant sprays it's still wise to cover the whole tree with plastic while it is being transported. Never leave it in hot sun. If no shade is available, dampen some cloth or burlap and shelter the plant with that. Black plastic will not protect a tree from direct sun; it absorbs heat and could cook your plant to death.

Once home the tree can be planted in a growing bed, large wooden box, or large pot, to be gradually shaped and trained after it recovers from the move. Treat it as you would any newly repotted plant.

NURSERY STOCK

It's easiest to work with a tree you have obtained in a nursery container. While shopping look for well-shaped trunk and main branches, thinking all the while of the basic shape that a particular tree suggests. It should be in reasonably good health, but since you don't want a perfect landscape specimen, you can

2–7 This tree is being root-pruned to develop fine roots close-in. The four solid lines represent the cuts made by thrusting a sharp shovel around the tree, severing about half the roots. The four dotted lines indicate cuts to be made the following year.
2–8 The third year the tree is carefully lifted, balled, and transplanted. Note trench-digging method, which keeps soil ball intact.

pay special attention to leggy, sparse, pot-bound plants that would not interest most buyers. Investigate the stock offered in the holding bins but then explore the back fields, the fringe areas, and behind the greenhouses where less comely plants may have been set aside.

One such search brought a very interesting specimen to my collection: a wisteria in a gallon can was found lying on its side in an abandoned sawdust bin. All the others had been sold and it had been left to its own devices. It had a fine, thick trunk and there were several branches within 2 feet of the can level. The top had vined 5 or 6 feet in all directions, and as we lifted the can, we discovered the roots had grown through the drainage holes and extended 17 feet along the subsurface of the surrounding composted sawdust. Tin shears were employed to cut away the half-rusted container and the roots were pruned to within a foot of the base (ground level) of the tree. The top was reduced by several feet, leaving two or three visible buds on each of three branches. This resulted in a tree about 28 inches high, ground level to top. A large training pot was used with a standard potting mix of one part loam, one part sand, and one part peat. (A heavier mix would have been adequate to the tree's needs but fine twig ramification was desired and sand encourages this.) The tree was set in a cool, shady place, the soil kept slightly moist, the top frequently misted.

The wisteria did not leaf out until July 10, later than normal, but then it began to grow well. Now, after two repottings it is a splendid specimen with an impressive trunk.

Most of the time when a badly root-bound plant is root pruned and repotted it responds with good growth. As small feeder roots develop the large, coarse ones can be removed, bit by bit, and progressively smaller pots can be used.

In the case described the plant was very kindly given to us by our friend the nurseryman, but even if you are shopping where you aren't known you may be able to secure a bargain, too. Ask if you can get the plant for a reduced price since it is not one of the owner's faster moving items. (Sometimes this is the understatement of the year!) This is a valid approach since the tree may not survive being moved.

Take your time when shopping for you may find a good possibility not immediately apparent. An old privet, cast aside from a landscape job, might be shaped into a beautiful, multiple-trunk style bonsai. A completely one-sided shrub, totally useless for landscaping, might make an interesting lightning-struck style, tilted to one side for a windswept style, or laid on its side and trained into a connected grove (raft style). Even a hefty six-footer can be given a tapered deadwood or jin tip, reducing its height by as much as several feet and taking advantage of a good broad trunk. Often you'll find nursery cans containing dead trees but filled with especially fine moss which is always very much in demand.

Sometimes you'll get gracious help and encouragement from nurserymen by mentioning that you're looking for bonsai material. Be prepared though for the salesman who sees you as an easy mark and offers worthless plants at ridiculous prices. It's best to enlist the owner or manager, who knows and appreciates plants and their possibilities. Unless the nurseryman is unusually well-educated it will be necessary to explain what you want and why. Few growers ever disturb the roots of a tree or shrub and most are aghast at the thought. Most of them are intrigued when introduced to the possibilities of bonsai, especially when they see how a waning plant can be restored to vigorous growth by root pruning.

It's a great help if the initial repotting can be done at the nursery, using the facilities (potting bench and soil) there. Bring along your own tools; it would be asking too much to borrow them, and besides, most nurseries use heavy-duty blade-and-anvil shears, which leave an unsightly stump.

The operation always becomes an impromptu "beginner's bonsai lesson," and one can evangelize for the art at the same time. Of course, your next trip to that nursery may reveal all the good plant possibilities have been taken by people you've converted!

The foregoing advice assumes that your shopping is being done during transplanting season. If it is not, keep your pre-bonsai plant growing in the pot until the proper season arrives or take it out of the pot and plant it in the open ground where you can either pot it in season or lift, prune, and replant in open ground for several years to let the tree more quickly reach the optimum size you prefer. If this is done, seasonal root and top pruning must not be overlooked; a tree or shrub in open ground develops so quickly it can soon grow entirely out of control.

The previous soil composition in which the plant was growing should be approximated at least for the first repotting of any plant. A too drastic change in growing medium can spell death for a newly acquired specimen.

BONSAI SUPERMARKETS

There is such a thing as a bonsai supermarket (figs. 2–9—21). It would be unfair to characterize all of them this way, but many of them are greenhorn traps. Such an establishment has been known to charge $500 for a poor old pine (see fig. 2–21) with heavy iron wires imbedded in the badly deformed and swollen trunk. These suppliers often have a full range of plants, adolescent and semi-finished bonsai as well as completed specimens which need only to be maintained.

In the main the supermarkets I've inspected were filled with very poor offerings. Many had been imported from Japan from careless or ignorant suppliers. You can differentiate this sort of supermarket from a reputable bonsai supply house by observing the quality of training and maintenance.

The supermarkets often do have some interesting accessories such as plateaus and figurines, and they usually sell tools, books, pots, and other equipment. Typical offerings include:

Moisture indicators (see Chapter 15)
Pruning paint—This is acceptable but experience recommends Elmer's glue or acrylic paint.
Vinyl mesh—Usually cheaper at your hardware store.
Bonsai fertilizer—Although some companies imply that you need only bonsai fertilizer, you should know that the fertilizer analysis *must* be tailored to the plant variety and age.
Bonsai potting soil—As with bonsai fertilizer one soil just won't do.
Pre-annealed copper training wire—You'll still have to anneal it shortly before use; in my experience, it always rehardens.
Artificial moss—This is really a pretty good idea. Sawdust dyed green and mixed with a small amount of glue works well. Pressed onto the surface of the soil, it helps retain soil contour, lets water through, and allows real moss or *Arenaria* to establish itself and finally take over. Watch to see that the artificial moss hasn't so much glue that a water-proof crust forms.
Turntables—Buy only a heavy turntable with a secure stoplock. Ignore the flimsy turntables which are sometimes offered. Instead of the latter, you'd do better with a

2-9 Small juniper grove (*J. chinensis procumbens nana*), 8 inches high, ready for wiring and further development. (*House of Bonsai, Naples, Florida*)

2-10 *J. procumbens*, 13 inches, basic style is well established. (*House of Bonsai*)

2-11 Small *J. procumbens*, 8 inches. (*House of Bonsai*)

24

2-12 This juniper could as easily have been trained into an upright style. This adaptability is one of the delights of the juniper family.

2-13 Italian cypress, 21 inches high, a very good subject for Zones 9–10.

2-14 Monkey puzzle (*Auracaria sp.*), 30 inches. Interesting display bench made of a slanting log with stair-step shelves cut in.

2-15 Sago Palm, 12 inches. *(House of Bonsai)*

2-17 Red mangrove showing typical stilt roots: three years in pot, tap water only, 21 inches. *(House of Bonsai)*

2-16 Red mangrove seedlings—an intriguing idea—15 inches high. *(House of Bonsai)*

2-18 Parsley aralia, 25 inches. *(House of Bonsai)*

2-19 Bonsai for sale.

2-20 Small boxwood, 9 inches.

2-21 A California bonsai supermarket had a $500 price tag on this one. The wires must have been in place for years; the tree was ruined.

plastic kitchen-cupboard turntable from the kitchen supply department of a department store.

In buying bonsai always be suspicious of a bargain. One grower attended an estate sale, and walking the grounds, he found a respectable bonsai collection on the terrace, all pieces marked for sale, Bargain! His joy evaporated when he found they were all dead or dying. They'd been left unattended by the executors, who had no notion of their considerable value.

Always shop around first to get an idea of price ranges. When you finally find the tree you want, only you can decide whether it's worth the money. If you like it that many dollars' worth and are sure you can keep it alive in your climate get all the history of the plant you can and take your treasure home. Never be too shy to ask questions. Ask how to care for it (feeding, pruning, training, repotting, soil mix, whether it requires sun or shade or wind exposure) and get the botanical name if possible so that you can research the subject yourself.

If you feel the price is too high you might tell the owner you love the tree but that you haven't the amount he's asking. Try bidding lower than the stated price. Some sellers will bargain.

A good bonsai is like a fine gem; it will cost money and one shouldn't expect to find a cheap one. A great deal of time, labor, devotion, and knowledge are involved in producing a handsome specimen; all of that is costly.

PROPAGATION METHODS

AIR LAYERING

Early spring, after the buds have begun to swell and loosen, is the best time to air layer (figs. 2–22,23). Make two cuts around the selected branch, completely girdling it (figs. 2–24,25). Depending on the thickness of the branch the cuts should be one to two inches apart. Remove the bark, including the cambium layer, and brush on a little rooting hormone. Rooting hormone is not a necessity and certainly the old bonsai masters didn't have such aids at their disposal, but it is helpful and often speeds the appearance of roots.

Wrap a large handful of moist, long-fibered spagnum moss over the exposed area, holding it close to the wood with a few turns of a rubber band which has been cut so that you may tie it in place. (The rubber disintegrates in a few weeks so there is no need to remove it when working with the new roots, which are delicate.) Wrap the mass of spagnum with clear plastic (fig. 2–26), folding it around two or three times and gathering it in on *each end* to form a moisture-tight seal. You may fasten the long side with tape if you like, but use rubber

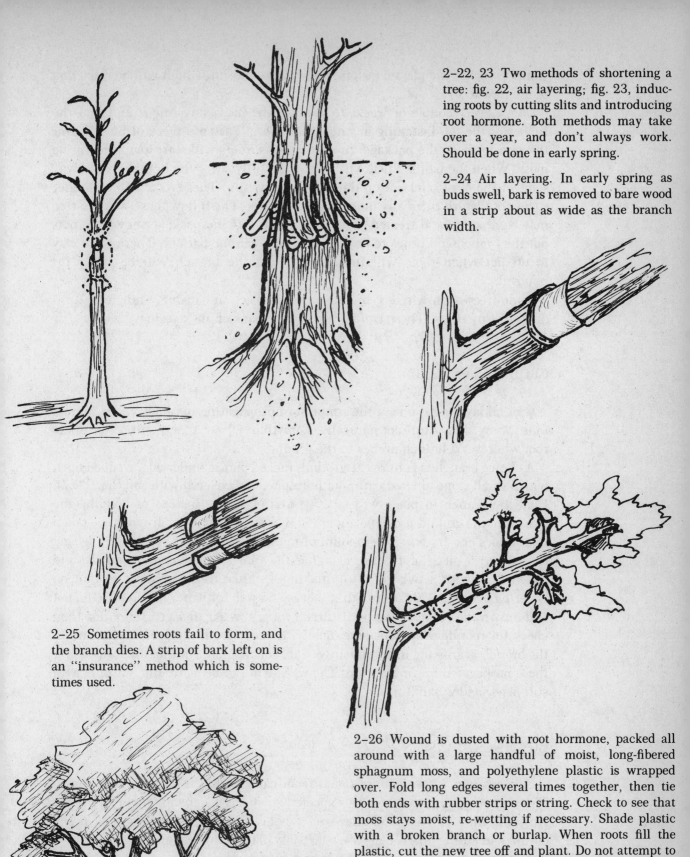

2–22, 23 Two methods of shortening a tree: fig. 22, air layering; fig. 23, inducing roots by cutting slits and introducing root hormone. Both methods may take over a year, and don't always work. Should be done in early spring.

2–24 Air layering. In early spring as buds swell, bark is removed to bare wood in a strip about as wide as the branch width.

2–25 Sometimes roots fail to form, and the branch dies. A strip of bark left on is an "insurance" method which is sometimes used.

2–26 Wound is dusted with root hormone, packed all around with a large handful of moist, long-fibered sphagnum moss, and polyethylene plastic is wrapped over. Fold long edges several times together, then tie both ends with rubber strips or string. Check to see that moss stays moist, re-wetting if necessary. Shade plastic with a broken branch or burlap. When roots fill the plastic, cut the new tree off and plant. Do not attempt to remove moss from the delicate new roots until the second transplanting, when straightening and arranging the roots will be all that is necessary.

2–27 Division, ground-layering. In each example a newly-rooted plant is severed from the parent at repotting time, when enough roots have formed.

bands to secure the plastic fastened just above the cut, which will be the trunk of the new tree.

Check every couple of weeks to see that the moss stays moist and that the rubber of the top fastening has not come loose. Fasten a piece of burlap over the area to shade the package. In a few weeks, roots will start to appear in the moss. When the ball is filled with roots, carefully sever the branch, pick away some of the moss, and pot up the tree in sandy soil. These roots will be tender so do not disturb them any more than necessary. The following season the tree may be repotted and treated as any other plant. If the package shows no roots but the branch continues to be healthy and green, be patient. There is no way to predict when roots will initiate or when the branch will be ready for removal.

Some trees form witches' brooms, a virus reaction causing a tangle of hundreds of tiny twigs. These can be rooted by means of air layering.

GROUND LAYERING

Ground layering is one of the simplest of propagating methods and it seldom fails. Many shrubs tip-root naturally. Forsythia, wisteria, and quince routinely root wherever a branch arches to the ground.

A choice branch is bent to the ground, nicked on the underside, wedged open with a small stone, dusted with root hormone, and covered with soil (fig. 2–27). Hold the branch in place with a crisscross of sticks. Instead of bending the branch to the ground it can be anchored in a pot of soil, but care must be taken that it does not dry out. The amount of maintenance can be reduced by setting the pot on a piece of plastic, bringing the plastic up over the branch, and fastening it with a twist of wire, making a miniature greenhouse so that no watering is needed. Make sure that there is no way for water to run into the pot and drown the roots. Leave undisturbed for six weeks to several months, then check for root development periodically. Remove from the parent plant when the branch is growing independently. Care for the plant in the same way as for those propagated by air layering. The roots will not be as fragile, but they will still need tender handling.

CUTTINGS, DIVISION

Cuttings (fig. 2–28, 29) are taken from early spring through late summer. The size of cutting that can be expected to succeed depends upon the plant type, the time of year, and the care it is given. For greatest success, make cuttings in spring when buds show activity. The stems should be semi-hard— just between the green flexible stage and hardwood.

For juniper, elm, maple, pine, and other plants native to the cooler climates the smaller twigs should be selected, from 1/16 inch to 3/4 inch in diameter. Tropical plants, such as the *Ficus* family, can often strike root from very large diameters, even several inches.

Make diagonal cuttings with a sharp knife. There should be at least three leaves or buds at the top and two empty leaf nodes or buds to insert beneath the soil. Dust the end of the stem (to just above the soil line) with root-hormone, make a hole in sandy soil, and insert the cutting. Pat down the soil gently to keep the cutting in place. The soil (2 parts sand, 1 part peat, 1 part loam) should be moist, not soggy.

Many plants can live for a long time on the reserve within the cutting itself without the support of roots, so don't disturb new cuttings until they show enough growth for you to be sure of a good root development. It's good practice, if the plants have been started in pots, to wait until roots start growing out of the drainage holes.

You can set the entire cutting and pot in a plastic bag (blow it up and tie the top tightly) or in a plastic shoe box with a lid. This makes it easier to control the moisture with difficult plants or especially large cuttings. Another good technique for moisture control with tiny single cuttings is to use two clear plastic drinking glasses, taped lip to lip. The cuttings can then be put under lights in the basement or wherever and forgotten until time to put them up. Keep them in a well-lighted, warm place (above 60° F. or 16° C.). The rooting medium should be kept moist at all times.

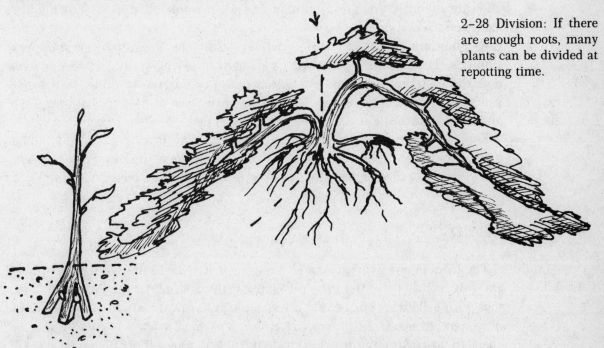

2-28 Division: If there are enough roots, many plants can be divided at repotting time.

2-29 Cuttings can be made of soft (green, limber) or hard woods (newly-developed woody twigs). Some zone 7 through 10 plants can be rooted from very large cuttings. Most hardwood trees will root from softwood cuttings taken in late spring, or hardwood cuttings made in winter or late fall.

To encourage taper, splits can be made and wedged open with ball of clay dusted with root hormone. Keep in moist, sandy soil in shade or under plastic in shade.

3. Training Seedlings and Young Plants

Several factors enter into the designing and training of young plants—the style should be natural to the type, pleasing to view, and not too difficult to maintain.

EARLY TRAINING OF DECIDUOUS TREES

Let's suppose we are working with several Chinese elm *(Ulmus parvifolia)* seedlings. We have ordered more than we intend to keep so that a wider choice can be had and any extras can be trained as trade, gift, or sale plants. If allowance is made for this, you may find it's possible to support your hobby—and even make a profit.

As they are unwrapped after delivery, sort the seedlings for style possibilities. The ideal is a plant with a straight, tapering trunk and feeder roots near the base (not just one long taproot). You can arrive at almost any design you want from this beginning. Elm is one of the best species for both beginner and master since the roots can be severely pruned.

Suppose you decide on one formal upright, one informal upright, and a grove. Training will be basically the same for all. You can select which ones to use for the specified styles when you see how each of the trees shapes up.

HEIGHT

The trees in our hypothetical group range between 15 and 18 inches (40–47 cm) tall, a little more than the ultimate height desired, so we will take off the tops with a slanting cut behind a leaf-bud (fig. 3–1). This will give rise to the new apex, at about 12 inches (31 cm). As each new apex begins to develop check to make sure it is growing straight up. If it takes off at an angle use small copper wire to hold it erect. Most of the time this topping cut produces an

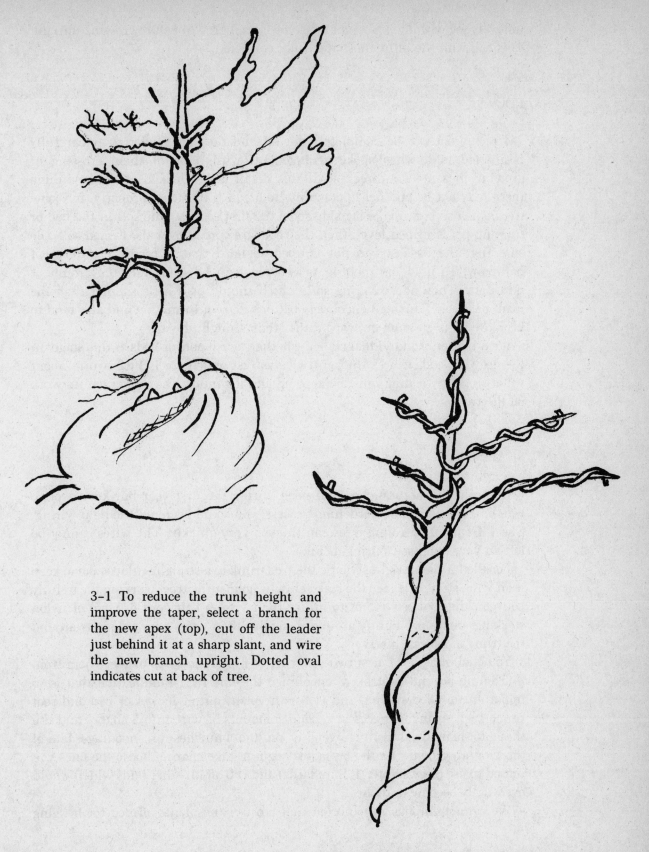

3-1 To reduce the trunk height and improve the taper, select a branch for the new apex (top), cut off the leader just behind it at a sharp slant, and wire the new branch upright. Dotted oval indicates cut at back of tree.

unlovely jog with the apex making some lateral growth before growing upright. This can ruin the ultimate shape if not corrected.

ROOTS

The taproot can be completely cut off and the side feeder roots carefully positioned in a wheel-spoke arrangement with none of them crossing or growing in a reverse direction. If this detail is overlooked at the beginning there may not be another opportunity to arrange the roots properly, for some trees, such as elm, make big side roots the first season. The soil in the bed or training pot is firmed level, then the roots are spread over the firmed soil. (Be sure that the base soil is not tamped so hard that it forms a waterproof hardpan.) To hold the roots in place twigs can be stuck into the ground if necessary. Then add covering soil, which should be a little sandier than the main base soil. This will encourage better side root formation and also tend to keep the roots growing outward rather than straight down.

It's a matter of individual choice whether to use pots or beds at this stage. In the growing bed, trunks thicken twice as fast and there is little worry about watering, but weeding must be kept up and it's much less convenient to work on the trees.

SHAPING

It's unlikely the branches will need wiring the first year but keep a close watch. If they start the hardening process, you could begin a little light wiring. Check frequently! Young trees can thicken very quickly. The wires cannot be left on very long (see Wiring, below).

For the formal upright style tie the tree trunk to a straight guide stake to keep it growing straight. Place the stake closely against the tree, working it carefully between the roots so as not to injure them. Use a soft cord or strip of nylon stocking, tie it once tightly around the stake, then wrap it more loosely around the trunk at several intervals.

Your main tasks the first two years are to nip branch tips to keep them from thickening beyond control, to encourage the fine twig ramification that is so important to good styling, and to lift the plant out of its pot or bed and root prune each spring. If necessary, bend some bits of wire into S shapes and use these to hang lead fishing weights on the branches to encourage lateral (horizontal) growth. As the branches begin to take shape, choose the ones you intend to use (see Chapter 1, Standards) and rub off all other buds which would eventually become branches.

We cannot emphasize too often that most of the plants offered for hedging (privet, mulberry, elm, wild plum, hedge-type maples, and Russian olive, to mention a few) tend to grow rampantly during their first several years. It's not uncommon for one of these to make a growth of 4 to 6 feet (1.2–1.8 m) in a single year if left uncontrolled.

We have been discussing the styling of elms, but these general suggestions apply to all deciduous trees. Consideration must be given to the characteristics of each species; you wouldn't prune a beech with as much reckless abandon as you might apply to an elm, for instance.

TRAINING EVERGREENS

Pines, spruce, junipers, and others will be treated with the same initial growing and training methods as deciduous trees (figs. 3-2—11). (See Chapter 11 for individual growing/training guidance.)

WIRING

Wiring is a simple process and one of the most important shaping methods. Copper wire is used as other types are too stiff or too soft or too prone to rusting quickly thereby staining and injuring the tree. Copper is not poisonous to trees. Unfortunately, it's fairly expensive at the hardware store and you can't always find the sizes you want. We asked an electrician friend to save unused lengths for us, and he presented us with a huge box of insulated wire of all gauges. After stripping off the insulation we had many dollars' worth of good wire ready for use.

To soften copper wire build a fire with small sticks in a charcoal grill and lay a few coils on the grill. When the fire burns down allow the wire to cool. Use immediately as it soon rehardens. You don't need a very hot fire; the Japanese use rice straw. Lacking a grill one could burn a few dry sticks in a cheap sheet-cake pan placed on the burners of a cook-top with the ventilator fan running.

There is a rule of thumb that usually holds true in determining the size of wire. If it is one-third of the diameter of a branch it will be strong enough for control. If it isn't, another wire can be applied neatly alongside the first one— but it should not overlap.

If the trunk needs control, use a length one-third longer than the distance to be wired. Place the wire beside the trunk, insert an inch or so into the ground, then coil the rest smoothly around the trunk—not too tightly but close enough for control. If the apex is too fragile for the gauge of wire you're using slip a piece of lighter gauge under the heavy wire, cut off the heavy wire, and continue up the trunk to the apex. Do not assume that the apex will grow upward without your help; wire it and tilt it slightly toward the front.

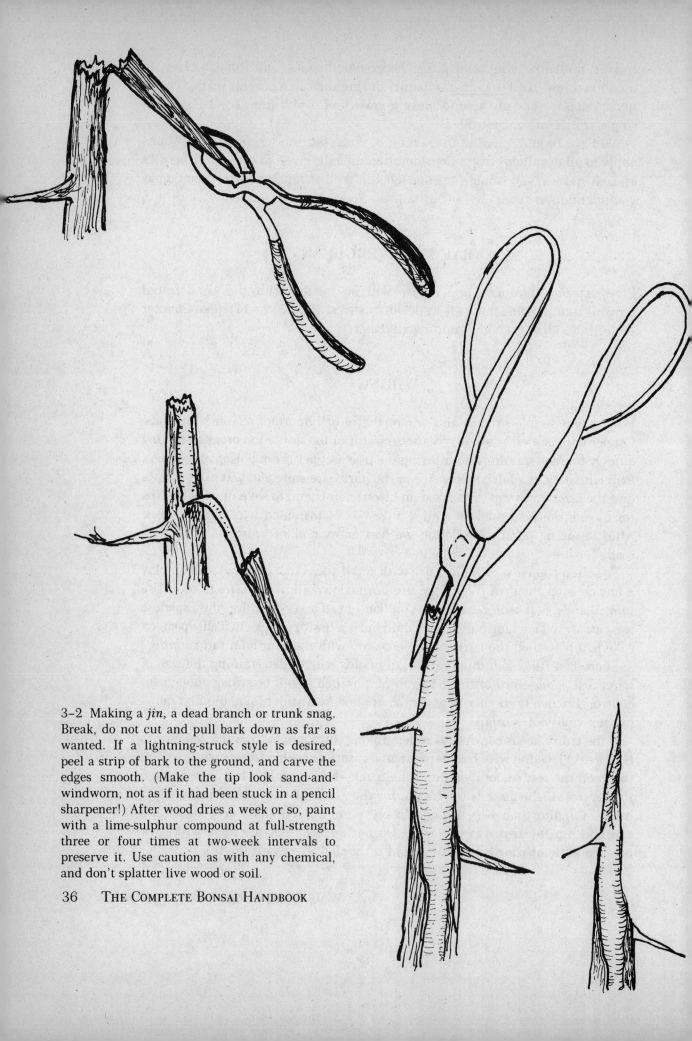

3-2 Making a *jin*, a dead branch or trunk snag. Break, do not cut and pull bark down as far as wanted. If a lightning-struck style is desired, peel a strip of bark to the ground, and carve the edges smooth. (Make the tip look sand-and-windworn, not as if it had been stuck in a pencil sharpener!) After wood dries a week or so, paint with a lime-sulphur compound at full-strength three or four times at two-week intervals to preserve it. Use caution as with any chemical, and don't splatter live wood or soil.

36   THE COMPLETE BONSAI HANDBOOK

3-3 Spruce branches can be cut back as far as is desired, so long as one or more buds are visible.

3-4 Spruce buds are elongating, pushing off their brown budcaps. It is still a little too soon for pruning tips.

3-5 Caps are just off, tassels are loosening. With tweezers, twist off center of each tassel leaving a few needles. Be careful; they may snap off completely if rough treatment is used. If a longer branch is wanted, let the tassel grow for a season.

3-6 One of the Japanese maple species. Pinch or cut back new twigs before they elongate fully.

3-7 These pine candles should be allowed to lengthen a little more before being broken off, leaving three or four needles on each candle base.

3-8 Cut back deciduous twigs, leaving one to three leaves.

3-9 If no new branch is wanted, buds on trunks should be rubbed off.

3-10 Pinch off new juniper buds.

3–11 Branch-benders should be used gently, tightening a little at a time, repositioning frequently.

As you work, hold the wire in place with the left hand (if you are right-handed) while pushing the spirals into place. Unless the branch is very hard and tough never use the branch to curve the wire; rather push the wire into place around it. Ideally, you should use such a gentle touch that you could wire an entire imaginary tree, leaving the wire to stand alone!

It's best not to coil wire around a whole tree and then bend the trunk and branches into place. Instead, as the wire is applied, gently guide each branch into the position you want. Minor adjustments can be made later.

Wherever possible, wire branches in pairs, using one wire for two branches (figs. 3–12, 13). Make a turn or two around the trunk to reach from one branch to another. Do not string wire through empty spaces; it doesn't hold well and looks sloppy. If all wires stay close to the tree they won't detract from its appearance.

Even bright, new copper wire soon oxidizes, taking on a dull hue that almost disappears on the bark of a tree. This is one reason trees can be exhibited with the wiring in place; if it's well done the appearance of the tree is not impaired.

LEAF PRUNING

A much finer tree is created if leaf pruning is carried out on a carefully planned schedule in the early part of its development. By late spring the leaves of most deciduous trees have matured and hardened off. This is the time to cut them off. The reason for this drastic (and sometimes dangerous) operation is to gain two year's twig development in one season. The trees manifest finer, more dense twigs and smaller leaves, and they have much better fall color.

Some trees can be leaf pruned more than once in a growing season. This depends upon the species, age, and vitality of the tree. Such species as beech, ginko, and oak will not generate new leaves unless the timing is very precise, with cutting done as early as the first leaves harden. Ordinarily they are not leaf pruned, nor are weak or sickly trees, nor needle evergreens, broadleafed evergreens such as holly and box, nor bearing-age fruit trees. Occasionally a

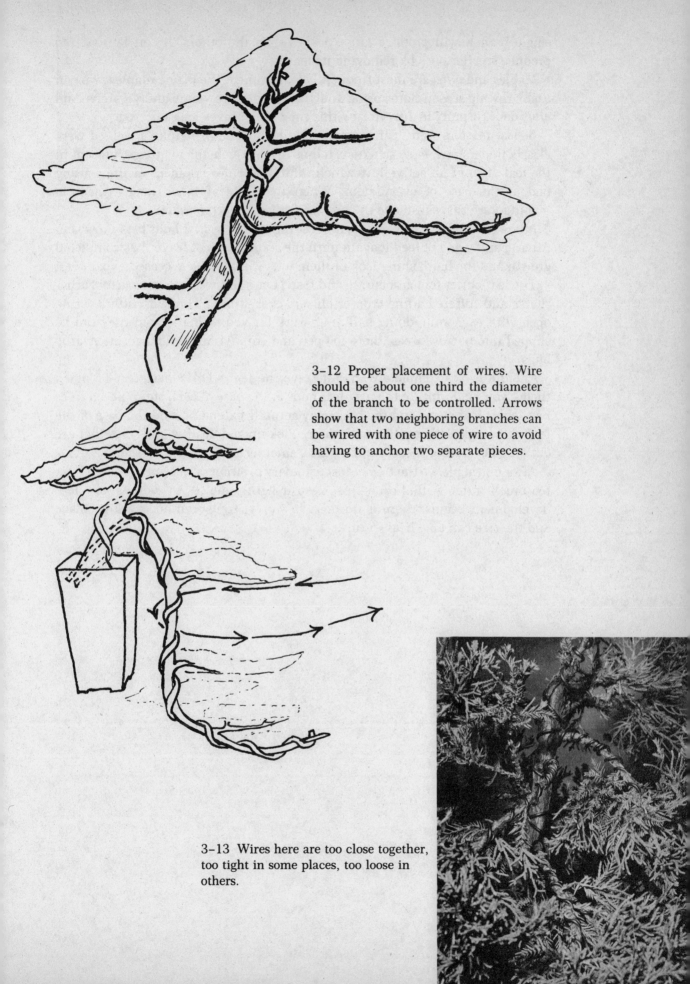

3-12 Proper placement of wires. Wire should be about one third the diameter of the branch to be controlled. Arrows show that two neighboring branches can be wired with one piece of wire to avoid having to anchor two separate pieces.

3-13 Wires here are too close together, too tight in some places, too loose in others.

single branch will produce larger leaves than the others. It can be made to produce smaller ones by removing its leaves.

Maples and elms are most frequently leaf pruned. We prune maples twice in each growing season (late spring and July) if they are young and vigorous, and elms once, usually in July, for by this time their leaves look tattered.

Bonsai masters were leaf pruning long before the principles involved were clearly understood. Now scientists tell us there is a chemical, *auxin*, present in the leaf stem of an active leaf which inhibits the development of the waiting bud at the base of every stem. When the old leaf is no longer there to manufacture this substance the bud immediately becomes active.

A tree should have its early spring feeding when the first buds begin to swell. After pruning do not feed it again until the second crop of leaves has completed growth and the hard, shiny look of them tells you they have ceased expanding.

The leaf-cutter tool is accurate and fast. (For years we used our trusty barber shears and suffered a fine crop of blisters every time.) The leaf cutters spring open with each snip, doing half your work for you. When closed they can be slipped into narrow areas, there to open and snip without endangering nearby buds.

Cut the leaves completely off but leave the leaf stem. Never tear or pluck them—you might injure the new leaf buds at the base of each stem. Beech trees have short leaf stems and the buds may actually extend beyond the base of the leaf, so be especially careful with them. Pick up and destroy all leaves that are cut off; they harbor insects and disease, smother moss, and look sloppy.

After cutting leave the tree in its customary position. Make sure it doesn't get too much water at this time—just keep it lightly moist. As soon as new leaf development begins, there is no need to worry; transpiration is taking place and the tree can take heavy rains.

4. Correcting Poor Style

Not every potential bonsai will have a style you like. It may be a fast-growing type that has simply become too coarse and long-limbed or your particular taste might see it in some other style, perhaps preferring an informal upright to be a slanting style, curved style, or even a cascade.

One is bewildered at the unlikely projects a bonsai master may adopt: "How can that spindly thing possibly become a bonsai? *I* certainly wouldn't want it!" The practiced eye of the master sees a bud here or a trunk taper there that can be encouraged, nurtured into a beautiful tree. It may be a heavy-trunked six-footer in a 5-gallon nursery can; the knowledge, talent, and—most of all—devotion of the grower can bring out imperceptible potential.

Ideally, fine bonsai are either collected in a near-finished design of nature or developed from seed through long years of methodical training, but the ideal is seldom encountered and there are exciting bonsai candidates everywhere.

MAKING A NEW APEX

In this picture series Joel is working with a large elm (figs. 4–1—4), *Ulmus parvifolia,* one of the best and easiest candidates for training. This one has been grown in a bed of rich, sandy soil, and though there are many well-placed branches and fine twigs, the upper trunk is much too thick and tall. We want one of the more slender upper branches to become the apex. So the top is sawed off, leaving several inches (in lieu of a stake) above the upper branch. The stake part is peeled to keep growth diverted from the old apex to the new one and a part of it is cut out to make room for the branch to be held as upright as possible.

Since elm is a very resilient wood this heavy branch will resist the new position and should be left in pads and training ropes for a year or more. As the branch, or new apex, expands its growth, the rope and pad are removed and retied to avoid marking the bark. This method is a good one for many types of

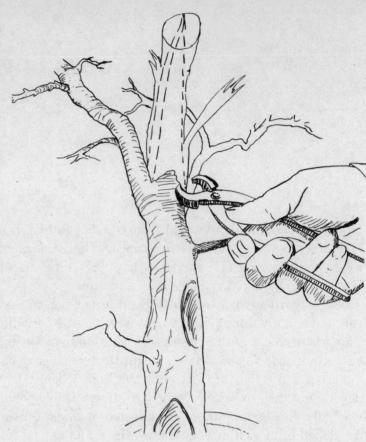

Joel Gold appraises possibilities of badly ~~ected~~ elm.

The old, thick top is sawed off, stripped, ~~tapered~~ to allow new apex (branch to the ~~~~ to be trained upright.

A piece of rubber-backed carpeting makes a ~~~~ pad to protect bark of new apex.

Though rather thick, the elm wood is re- ~~~~nt enough to be pulled upright in one ~~~~ration.

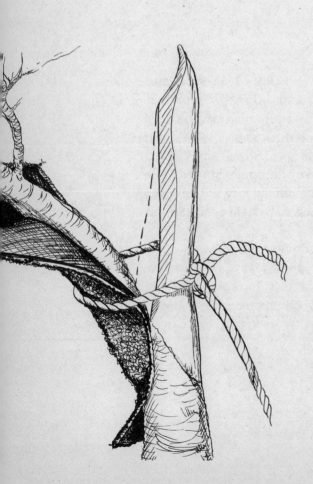

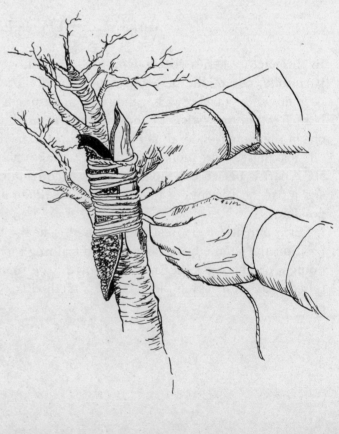

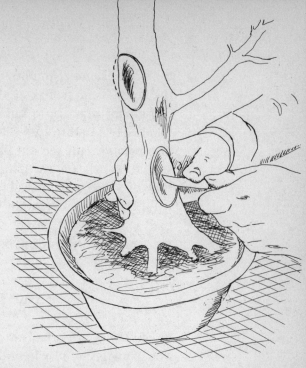

4-5 Old pruning wounds are carved smooth at edges and hollowed slightly for faster, flatter healing.

4-6 Dotted line shows previous contour.

4-7 There's much to be done toward training this tree, but taper has been improved and height reduced. Binding may remain for several months, then replaced a time or two until the new position is adopted permanently. The old apex will be removed when it is no longer needed as a stake.

4-8 This elm received similar training the previous year.

4-9 The bark is beginning to close over the wound where the old apex was removed.

trees and is one of the best ways to reduce the height of a tall tree or improve the taper of the trunk.

It's poor practice to cut off a tree and leave a stub even if it's hidden by foliage for a square stub seldom heals properly. When the new apex accepts its new position, the old one should be cut off at a slant behind it and the wound should be concave so that healing will be flat. Always place large cuts at the back of a tree when possible (figs. 4–5, 6).

When an elm or maple is pruned heavily the surrounding bark sends out buds which distort the area. To avoid this tape wound edges securely and leave the tape on until healing begins (figs. 4–7, 8, 9).

CREATING THE BROOM STYLE

Broom styles are often developed from rather large trees (figs. 4–10, 11, 12). The trunk is cut off where the base of the broom-pattern branching is to be and firmly wound with wide rubber strips to make the branches fan out gracefully from the trunk. Without the binding a swollen snarl develops, destroying the style. Notice the cut is not straight across (see figs. 4–10, 11).

As the branches lengthen they are pinched back repeatedly to encourage fine twigs to form. An impressive, large-trunked broom style can be formed in just a few years. This is a style often employed for zelkova, or Japanese grey bark elm.

4–10 For a broom style elm or zelkova the cut is made in an asymmetrical V, then hollowed as shown, making a little bowl. 4–11 Cut end is bound with tape or rubber strips to prevent swelling. Choose three, five, or seven twigs and prune as shown. Cut out others. Buds on trunk are rubbed off. 4–12 The following season. The tape has been removed. Pruning will be continued as shown to develop fine twigs.

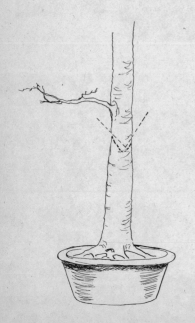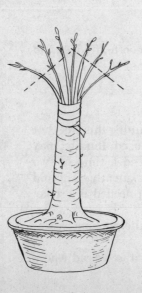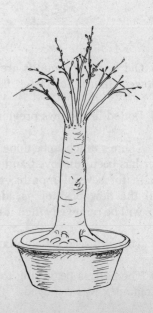

5. Instant Bonsai—Creating a Tree to Enjoy Today

A tree can often be given a bonsai pot of the proper size from the beginning. When this happens it is fun, for you will have the reward of your labors immediately, a rare thing in any endeavor (figs. 5-1—3).

Junipers of all kinds, dormant deciduous trees and shrubs, and many pines and spruces are good possibilities for instant bonsai (figs. 5-4—9). We'll use an upright juniper for our example. It has a nicely tapered double trunk, and enough limbs to select from for a pleasing formal upright style (fig. 5-10). Your exploring fingers dig into the topsoil and find some promising surface roots radiating out from the trunk in a fairly even pattern. Careful planning now means the difference between a tree you will be proud of, and failure.

FIRST DECISIONS

With one hand over the surface soil turn the pot upside down. If the soil ball does not fall out tap the edge of the pot on a firm surface. (We use a D-handle shovel which has been driven into the ground. The wooden handle doesn't break clay pots and there is a minimum chance of injuring branches, as you might on a table edge.) You may be pleased to discover that the plant is growing in the top portion of the soil ball and can easily do without so much soil. But you may find that the roots have completely filled the container and have run in circles around the bottom. In this case, the lower roots may be in a black, nonfunctioning condition, if they are not already dead.

When there is such a small root development that you don't have to prune much to fit the root ball comfortably into the pot, you can choose whether to remove top growth or leave it, depending on the style shape you choose. With a rootbound tree you *must* remove enough top growth so that the tree can survive loss of some of the roots. It's reasonably safe to remove one-third of the roots

5–1 A tiny *Chamaeciparis obtusa.*   5–2 The soil is filled with roots. The small six-sided pot at the right front is chosen, and roots and top pruned.   5–3 Pruned and wired, with potting almost done. Pruning wounds will be painted with a color to hide and protect them.

and one-third of the top of a juniper, pine, or spruce, and one-half or even more of a dormant deciduous tree. Make sure that plenty of fine feeder roots are present. You wouldn't be safe taking the few heavy roots of oak and beech trees, for instance.

The juniper we are working with has a soil ball completely packed with roots. Digging away the topsoil we find good surface roots an inch below the surface, giving a slightly longer trunk-base than first appeared. We decide that the height will remain about the same for the style we want but that one-third of the branches and about the same amount of roots will be thinned out. *Replace the tree in its pot.*

BRANCH SELECTION

Start now from the base of the tree and select the primary branch. It should be the largest, thickest side branch of the completed tree and should be placed about one-third of the way up the planned height of the trunk. Mark it with chalk or a piece of masking tape. On the opposite side, choose a slightly higher branch and continue up the trunk, finding a basic shape. Mark enough back branches to keep the tree in balance and give it depth: Don't overlook the importance of these back branches. Side and front branches are chosen to expose and frame the trunk. Look at the tree frequently from above to be sure the front doesn't become flat. Thin and wire the branches to complement the trunk and achieve the chosen style and shape while giving the impression of an old, mature tree.

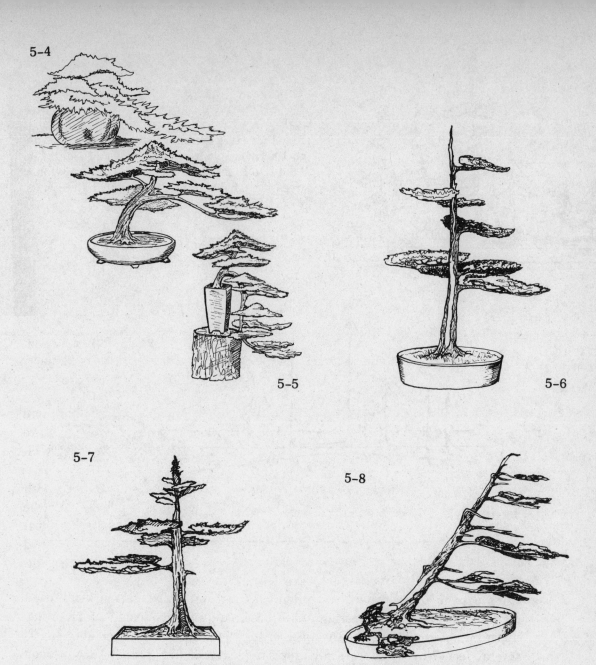

5-4,5 Three possible styles to be had from a large nursery grown *Juniperous procumbens* (see figs. 3-12, 13 for wiring details).

5-6 It's amazing to see how a neglected derelict from a nursery back lot can revive when proper pruning of top and roots is done. The few branches show a tenacity for life—a trait we can encourage.

It can be designed as a lightning-struck style (see fig. 3-2).

5-7 Shortened even more for a hollow-trunk style (for apex treatment, see fig. 3-1).

5-8 Slanted to one side for a windblown style with a tiny *J. procumbens nana* as a companion (and for balance).

5-9 Raft style. Trunk is slit and wedged with root-hormone dusted balls of clay and planted in sandy soil. Branches are wired as individual trees—root ball is cut off at dotted line when roots form beneath the new trees.

It's easy to forget where you intended the front to be, so mark it. After marking the branches that seem to fill these requirements decide which of the upper branches will become the apex, or highest point. Mark it and stand back several feet. How is the overall proportion? Is the first branch at a proper height? Is one side too much heavier than the other? Stand above, and look down. Do the branches radiate from the trunk in a reasonably well-balanced pattern? Throughout your work make a habit of standing back for evaluation the way an artist does with a painting. If the general impression is not what you had in mind—perhaps you estimated the wrong height or a different primary branch should be tried—remove the markers and begin again.

Once you are satisfied with your design make certain all potting materials are at hand, including slightly moist potting soil. Mix tepid water and Transplantone or some other transplanting preparation at the recommended strength (no stronger) in a container large enough to accommodate the pot just to the rim. Cut vinyl screening to cover drain hole. Broken pot chards take up

5-10 This is young nursery stock, 2-gallon size. We looked for good rootage well distributed around base, tapering trunk, and enough branches to form interesting pattern. 5-11 Comb out roots and soil with chopstick, blunt pencil, or (shown) that famous tool and weapon of the dockworker, the cargo-hook. Prune roughly as many roots as branches.

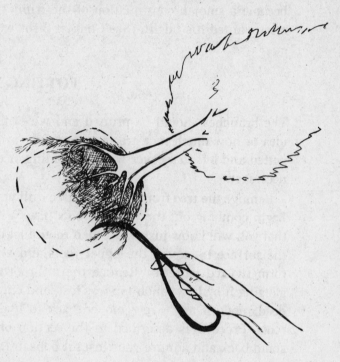

too much room, where every fraction of an inch counts, and let soil leak out and insects in.

BRANCH PRUNING

Begin gradually to prune unwanted branches; if you are uncertain about any branch try masking it off with a piece of cloth to get an idea of how the tree looks without it. After pruning spray the entire foliage mass with Wilt-Proof or some other anti-dessicant. This is not absolutely necessary, but it is good insurance. Remove the tip of the tree behind the branch that is to be the new apex. Cut at a slant to encourage taper. Paint all wounds on trunk and branches with acrylics to match the bark for a neat, finished look. If you use two or three shades of color daubed on in blotches you can disguise new cuts very well. Do not extend paint onto bark.

WIRING

Cut a length of wire approximately one-third longer than the distance to be wired, anchor it in the soil at the back of the trunk, coil it around the trunk, and continue coiling to the primary branch that you wish to shape. It may not be necessary to wire all branches but the apex must be wired to stand erect and slightly angled toward the front. If it is left to grow untended, it will not become a smooth continuation of the trunk but will show a crook where you most wanted it straight. (See Chapter 3 for wiring diagrams.)

POTTING

The branches should be pruned and wired first so that you will have a good idea of how much root area can be safely pruned away. Then the tree can be potted and left to recover without jostling or exposing the roots any more than necessary.

Remove the tree from the pot with a dull pencil, tapered stick, or cargo hook. Begin combing out the tangled roots (fig. 5–11); they must be straightened so that you will know just how much root must be dealt with. Brush off the soil at the surface to expose the upper roots and untangle or trim any that cross or form twisted patterns. Reduce the soil-root mass by about one third or less, gauging it by how much top was lost, and cut off surplus roots. The blackened, dead roots, if any, are removed back to live tissue to encourage new feeder roots. Proceed as described in the section on repotting in Chapter 12. Then stand back and admire your instant bonsai! (fig. 5–12).

5-12 Branches have been pruned and wired, and guided into the configurations of an old, mature tree. Root mass will be further reduced in the future, and leaves will become more dense with pruning and training. An hour or two of work has produced a very attractive specimen, which may someday become a true bonsai!

6. Evaluating Possibilities of Individual Plants

No matter what name a plant bears, the only criterion to keep in mind when considering it for bonsai is: Will it look right? The plant should have leaves that are naturally small or should dwarf well with pruning and potting, short spaces between leaf buds, interesting bark, and it must withstand confinement in a container. If it also offers flowers, fruit, and/or good fall color, then we are considering an interesting bonsai possibility. After this, the main problem will be to give the plant the growing conditions it demands.

ACCENT PLANTS

We have been discussing candidates for bonsai only. In your arrangements you will also want accent plants to add interest and variety. Thousands of such plants are available and are used to establish a theme or define a season in an exhibit. (A fruiting strawberry plant would indicate midsummer, for instance.) The need for variety becomes evident when we realize that a pine or spruce, no matter how fine the tree, looks very much the same whatever the season.

GROUND COVER

Ground-cover plants lend beauty to arrangements and they also keep the soil cool and hold moisture in place during rain or watering. On the negative side ground covers often have voracious roots which invade the growing space of the bonsai and rob it of nourishment. Watch out for this and remove any too-enthusiastic growers. It's even wise to thin out the less rampant ones occasionally to make sure the tree gets all the air it needs. There is more about accent plants and ground covers in Chapter 9.

6–1 An old multiflora rose plant, with a large trunk and branches and roots many feet long, is reduced top and botton in the early spring. Notice the slanting cut is made at the back of the trunk (dotted line) in order to establish a taper. New buds soon appear, and a few at the top are selected for training.   6–2 Presenting the cloud style!

POSSIBILITIES OF EACH TREE

In choosing your candidate for bonsai, think of the future. Does the tree have a long life expectancy? Most pines, oaks, zelkovas, beeches, and junipers are long-lived. Or is it known to be a short-lived tree? The faster growing trees (including poplars, soft maples, and willows) tend to have shorter lives. This does not mean they are completely undesirable, but life-expectancy is one consideration in choosing a tree.

Always keep the future in mind while you plan your course of action. Decide what shape you want your tree to have and look for small buds where you think a new branch should grow (figs. 6–1, 2). Bud grafting is not difficult, but if you can find a tree with existing potential, so much the better. Some trees, such as azalea, rose, and Scotch pine, will sprout buds even on severely cut-back branches. Others, like black pine and oak, are unlikely to do this and the branch will probably die if cut back beyond visible buds.

One of the reasons we should familiarize ourselves with all the bonsai styles is to widen our viewpoint. A tree with only a few branches at the very top could be a complete dud or it might be developed into a striking example of the *literati* style. Success is almost completely within the hands of the grower, depending upon his or her imagination, knowledge, and discrimination.

Rather than deciding "I want this juniper to be a cascade," look at the plant from every angle. Turned on its side and wired upright, it might make a superb formal upright style. Look at each tree with an open mind. It's true that in bonsai the grower can mold a plant to almost any form, but it is equally true, and exciting, that there are almost endless possibilities in every plant (fig. 6–3).

6–3 This two-year-old cork oak *(Quercus suber)* appears to have little promise; certainly none of the standard one, two, and three points are in evidence. After wiring and bending to the basic design, the young tree is given a wide shallow pot to encourage broad surface roots. Watch closely, and remove wires before they become too snug. Rewire when necessary. The pot should be large, leaving plenty of room for development. The soil surface is not raised above the rim of the pot—every effort is made to keep roots comfortable and growing. The tree is consistently overpotted each year. This oak is asymmetrical, so a little extra pot space is allowed on the heavy side, for balance.

When growth slows and the trunk and branches assume the planned shape, smaller pots are employed. The restricted soil mass slows growth, shortening internodes. The tree then begins to harden, bark shows more character, roots thicken, and a maintenance schedule is launched.

7. Terrains

Once the idea of miniaturizing trees and shrubs is conceived it naturally follows that those trees could become part of a little patch of countryside—a landscape arrangement.

GROVES

Most groves are of one species of tree—almost any tree suitable for bonsai can be used. The overall effect should be one of harmony. If stones are included they should be of the type normally seen with the kind of trees that make up the grove. One should not use rugged seaside rocks with a trident maple grove, or smooth, low-profile stones with wind-whipped juniper planting.

Special pots are made for the grove style; they are long, very low, and seldom have any decoration. They may be oval, round, rectangular, primitive free-form or, as in the case of Kawamoto trays, have two or more compartments—one for a planting and one for a lake which can contain bog plants as well as water. Most containers have drainage holes (see Chapter 14, Making Bonsai Containers) but sometimes the trees are planted on rocks with the roots confined to soil pockets and not extending into soil below. Such plantings are often made in *suibans*, low trays which have no drainage holes. Damp sand or water is then kept in the *suiban*.

To develop a convincingly realistic grove, study your best teacher, Nature. The most attractive groves usually feature one dominant tree with others clustered around it at varying distances. Few will be the same height. The same principles that dictate the shape of one tree apply to a group of trees. The search for light, moisture, air, and space affects the placement of leaves and branches at strategic levels (see fig. 1–10). The trees are best shaped in separate pots, not integrated into a group until well along in training.

DESIGNING THE GROVE

The soil should exhibit a gently rolling profile; there would be little variety or interest if the grove were on a perfectly flat plain. Place the dominant tree off center, somewhere toward the front of the tray. It should be on a rise—probably on the highest mound of soil. Arrange the other trees around the focal tree. Stand back frequently to make sure that the grouping is natural, with no trees standing in stiff, unnatural straight lines, or one directly behind the other. If stones are to be used position them at the same time as the trees; never just lay them on top of the soil as an afterthought. The composition will be more stable and the stones will look far more authentic if partially buried. Do not use stones unless they are truly a part of the impression you wish to produce; many beginners drop a few stones here and there without reason.

Do not fill the entire tray with trees; leave open areas to walk through (in fantasy!) and enough space around the edges to give proportion and make the grove look comfortable. Often a double grove is effective, with one dominant tree flanked by lesser trees, a space indicating a wide path or a narrow meadow, then another group of trees that are similar to the first but usually smaller in scale.

POTTING

Spread the roots and cover the soil, firming well as you would in any repotting. Work soil among the roots. Make certain all the trunks are at the same angle. If they tilt all different directions they will look artificial and awkward. This is not to say they should not have individual curves and bends, but there must be a plan, a theme. Do the subsidiary trees lean slightly away from the main tree? Is the one huge tree flanked by its offspring? In this case the parent tree would be much larger and the others would be dominated by it to such an extent they would be leaning away in search of light. Or are all the trees in the grove about the same age? Then one would expect to see many tall, slim trunks all growing up at the same angle. The larger trees should be put to the front, with the smaller ones at the back to emphasize the impression of depth and distance. A grove of junipers on a windy crag would all grow in the same direction, moulded by the prevailing winds.

TYING DOWN THE TREES

If any of the trees need tying down to hold them steady, use natural-fiber binder twine or hemp (available at hardware stores, hatcheries, or farm-supply stores). It will disintegrate in a few months and will not girdle or mark the roots. Run it up through the drainage holes (and through the vinyl screening covering the holes) and tie in place. If wire is used it must be removed before it can injure the roots, is sometimes hard to locate, and its removal may disturb any surface covering such as moss.

REPOTTING

Once established, the grove is repotted as one unit—the individual trees are not separated again. A very old grove becomes more and more beautiful as surface roots intertwine and unite.

SAIKEI

A more fanciful adaptation is *saikei,* which can be a group of trees, shrubs, rocks, and sand, or one tree with rocks, sand, and a few tiny shrubs and underplantings. The saikei, or "living landscape," attempts to create a whole natural scene in miniature. Small in-scale figures of people, animals, boats, houses, and bridges may be used but their arrangement should be spare and subdued. It is far better to present a sketchy suggestion with a few well-placed objects than to contrive an over-produced epic.

IDEAS FOR SAIKEI

One of the most effective saikei involves one windswept juniper on an island (a mound of green moss) with a few jutting rocks (suggesting a sturdy base for the island) and surrounded by lapping ocean waves of fine sand. The stones all are oriented the same direction as if part of one massive formation.

Another fine example utilizes fifteen tiny formal upright junipers of varying sizes growing upon a cliff composed of carefully arranged stones. There is a moss-carpeted cleft running diagonally through the planting, suggesting a split in the rock formation. Parts of the cliff jut out at intervals. The trees stand at random levels as if sown there by the wind. A waterfall can be suggested by placing light colored sand in a rock declivity. It can descend to the lowest level, where a pool can be represented by fine sand surrounded with moss and tiny shrubs.

The saikei style gives an opportunity to use a variety of plants. One large tree, an old boxwood, accompanied by profusely flowering miniature roses makes a pleasant sight. *Acoris, selaginella,* wild thyme azalea, mosses of different varieties—an endless array of small plants can be integrated into a terrain. They should be grouped rather than scattered about. It's natural to find clusters of plants and trees which have spread to occupy a specific area. All plants in a saikei should be compatible as to maintenance requirements (figs. 7–1, 2, 3). There is an extra bonus in saikei; when the trees become too large, they may be repotted and made into individual bonsai.

ROCK PLANTING

Rock planting can be some of the most dramatic of all bonsai. The image of a few tenacious junipers and wild thyme azaleas clinging to the face of an almost vertical cliff invokes thoughts of courage and strength. A rock with many rugged, jagged angles is best. The plants are installed in a pocket of tacky, sticky soil on the crag. They will not be repotted in the usual sense, but the soil can be picked away from the surface and replaced occasionally.

MAKING A ROCK PLANTING

Mix equal parts of brown sphagnum moss, black Michigan peat (milled), and loam. Add enough water to make it stay together in a ball and knead it until it is a cohesive mass. This soil (it's called muck) has been pressed and mixed until all air is expelled, which is contrary to everything we have learned about planting mediums. It's necessary to do this so that the medium will stay where it is put, however.

Pack some soil where the tree is to go and spread the roots over it. To furnish a little aeration pat grains of perlite or vermiculite over the roots, then follow with the soil mix again. If there is not enough of a depression in the rock to accommodate the tree roots without assistance, fasten holdfasts to the stone before beginning to place the tree. The usual method is to pound bits of lead (from fishing supply stores or aquarium shops) over copper wire, forcing enough lead into crevices to hold the wire. The new epoxy glues also can be used. Cut a length of wire and a small patch of vinyl screening and glue the wire down, using the patch over it for reinforcement. Continue with the planting. If the screening bulges slightly here and there it furnishes a better grip for the developing roots. As the tree is positioned it is loosely wired into place with the holdfast wires. Leave enough room for developing roots. You can put a pad of sphagnum moss between root and wire.

Once the tree is securely fastened in place and roots are covered with muck, finish with moss which can be held in place with small staples of wire.

7-1 Terrain with *Cryptomeria*, cotoneaster, wild thyme azalea, *salagenella* and moss, 21 inches long. All these plants grow well in a bright location on the coffee table the year round, except for a 2-month stay in a cool garage (October, November). Without the cool rest, the azaleas would not bloom.

7-2 It's fun to find rocks that will be the basis for a terrain or rock planting as shown in this closeup of the previous photo. (*Dunton collection*)

7-3 Terrain with small junipers and wild thyme azaleas, 23 inches long. This one can stay for several weeks at a time in the house, but is better put outside most of the time.

Do not allow the planting to dry out; water gently with a fine spray of water or use the drip method of watering (see Chapter 15).

Keep in the shade for two weeks, gradually giving more sun until it is getting lightly dappled shade (depending upon the type of plant, of course). This planting should not have full sun unless your watering schedule is unusually faithful; one hour in hot sun can destroy a beautiful planting (figs. 7–4, 5).

7–4 Trident maple (*Acer burgerianum*), planted on a rock. Fine twig ramification brought about by yearly leaf-pruning.

7–5 This distant-mountain stone gives mood and depth to the composition. (*Ann Pipe collection. Dunton photo*)

8. Grooming

Good grooming is a prerequisite for every living thing. Health and self-respect demand a level of maintenance that includes cleanliness, neatness, and organization. A neglected tree reflects the owner's attitudes, just as a well-kept, neat tree indicates the life habits of its keeper. For the very best health and growth, keep your trees free of debris, dead twigs and leaves, and pests.

DAILY GROOMING STEPS

Ideally, grooming should be a daily concern (see Chapter 15, General Care). To prepare a tree for a show, a little more consideration is given to the overall cosmetic details. Look at the entire unit—tree, ground cover or soil surface, and pot. Strive for the neatest, most polished effect possible. Try to picture how it would look to a person seeing it for the first time. Never mind that the ground cover grows so fast you can't keep it trimmed or that there are probably too many long twigs you haven't gotten around to cutting and thinning. Reject excuses and be objective.

REMOVE DEAD MATTER

Clip, don't pull, any dead or discolored leaves. Old, brown pine or spruce needles can be pulled. Remove spent flowers and old fruit.

WEED

Pull any weeds, even very small ones. Bonsai tweezers are useful for this job;

they can reach down and get the whole plant, leaving no roots. You may have to place your fingers on either side of the weed to keep the surface from being disturbed. If there is no vegetation covering the soil, brush it free of any large, dry clods or other distractions and give a top dressing of fine, dark soil.

TRIM GROUND COVER

Clip any over-long bits of ground cover or moss. Ground covers should not spill over the edge of the pot unless that is how you especially plan it. Occasionally a modest drape of *Arenaria* might be attractive, but be discriminating about allowing this.

CLEAN THE POT

Remove mineral deposits from the pot with steel wool, scrubbing cloth, or vinegar water and smooth a little baby oil over the edges where most deposits occur. A very thin coat of oil could be applied to the entire pot—*very thin,* since you don't want to seal the clay so that no transpiration can take place. Furniture wax can also be used. Never put oil on the tree itself. If there is mineral deposit on the trunk treat it very gently with a half-and-half mixture of white vinegar and water. Apply it with a cotton-tipped swab, then rinse.

BRANCH CLEAN-UP

Remove any webs or other debris from the branches. If a leaf or twig seems to detract from the design, clip it off. The same goes for over-large leaves.

LOOK UNDER THE POT

Clean under the pot, checking to see that no pests hide there and that the drain holes are not stopped up by roots. Cut off any roots found growing through the holes.

CHECK FOR INSECTS AND DISEASE

Make it a habit to look for insects and indications of disease. A bad infestation often can be obviated by apprehending the first few invaders.

SHOWER THE TREE

Finally, give the whole tree and pot a cleansing shower. If there seems to be any scum residue left from insecticides or deposited when dew falls on dusty leaves, spray with a light solution of liquid detergent (approximately a half teaspoon to a quart of water), then rinse well with clear tepid water.

And there it stands: face washed, shoes polished, and hair slicked back—well, figuratively at least—ready to be seen and admired!

9. Accent Plants and Ground Covers

IDEAS AND SUGGESTED PLANTS

Accent plants are used to soften the stark simplicity of a single bonsai or to establish a season. A clump of *Galanthus* in a small tray at the foot of a dignified old pine would indicate early spring or a robust, blooming dandelion near an elm in full leaf says "It's midsummer!" Any flower, shrublet, vine, grass, or small tree that complements your bonsai and is in scale is eligible. It may be planted with your bonsai or in a separate pot. You might like to use dwarf river rush near a grove of black birches to imply the coolness of nearby water. Flowering and bearing alpine strawberry plants in a large saikei tray are marvelous on a summer dining table, or as a single companion to a hackberry, bringing forth dreams of a meadow's edge where wild strawberries sprawl at the feet of the tall trees (figs. 9–1—4).

To decide whether a plant is suitable as a ground cover for bonsai consider these points: Does it stay in scale? Will its roots compete? Will it spread evenly to make a uniform background for my tree? Not many species meet all these criteria, but new types are always being tried, and it's intriguing to look for more. The accent plant idea is fun, and the possibilities are unlimited! Some of the types of plants are listed below along with suggestions for their care. The zones refer to the United States Department of Agriculture Hardiness Zone Map (Chapter 15).

ACORUS *(Gramineus minimus)*: Zones 7-10, sometimes 5-6. Small accent plant good in saikei or terrains.

This is a tiny irislike plant 1-2 inches tall (2.6-5.1 cm) and very attractive whether all green or in its variegated form.

9–1 Alpine strawberry and grape vine, 20 inches long. *(Dunton collection)*

Location
  Almost a bog plant, needs plenty of water.

Light
  Grows well in most light exposures, but may get brown edges in midsummer sun.

ARENARIA *(Arenaria balearica*—say ar-e-ná-rea): **Zones 5–10. Ground cover.**
  This plant has many common names including alsine, Scotch or Irish moss, and sandwort. The common names go on and on, bringing confusion and

9–2 An Alpine strawberry blooms and bears all summer in its 2-inch pot.

9–3 Miniature roses have flowers in fine scale for larger terrains and as companion plants. This one is named "Small World" and blooms throughout the season.

9–4 *Ficus pumila* growing at the roots of *Ficus benjamina*. Leaves less than ½ inch long.

9-5 Dwarf red iris complements young Alberta spruce.

9-6 Dwarf yellow iris.

disappointment to anyone attempting to buy this delectable little plant without using its botanical name. There are also many species of this plant family, some too large for our use, so always order it by its exact botanical name.

These perfect little grassy plants begin as a symmetrical thread-leaved plant under half an inch (1.3 cm) high. Tiny creeping stems radiate out to establish more plants, and soon the ground is covered with the best miniature grass effect imaginable. Diminutive white flowers open from May through July. Arenaria is ideal for ground cover around the trunk of a fine old pine, or to sod the meadow of a saikei (figs. 9–7, 8).

Soil

Use any good soil but make sure it will drain well as the plants cannot survive standing water.

Light and feeding

Grows well in most light intensities and thrives upon whatever you choose to feed the saikei or bonsai it's keeping company with.

BROMELIAD *(Tilansia sp.):* Zones 9–10. Saikei accent.

Looking like minuscule gray-green yucca plants, some of the bromeliads are tiny and can remain under one-half inch indefinitely. We have had several of the smallest ones for five years, and growth has been extremely slow, less than one centimeter a year. The tiniest one was so small it perched for two years in the boughs of an ivy *mamé,* where we could only find it by knowing where to look. Its only requirement during this time was dappled shade and a drop of water in its crown daily.

The plant now resides on a tiny pad of *osmunda fiber,* which is anchored on the soil at the base of the ivy. It is the size of my thumbnail, after five years! We moved it to the *osmunda* because we thought it needed a permanent toe-hold, but it still has not anchored itself, even though it continues to grow.

Size and position

Bromeliads may be from microscopic to bushel-basket size. They usually are found firmly clasping rough-barked branches, occasionally falling with dead branches to the ground, where they may continue to grow.

Light

Dappled sun and shade and good air circulation are necessities.

Feeding and watering

Our tiny bromeliad was given a daily drop of water in its crown, and every

9-7 *Arenaria* in bloom—see the minuscule flower at the tip of my index finger?

9-8 *Arenaria* and moss growing on a rock.

six weeks one-fourth strength Hyponex, Rapid-Gro, or Schultz Liquid Fertilizer was added to the water. A daily misting is beneficial. Bromeliads must be kept upright so that the cuplike crown can be filled with water at all times.

Winter protection

Protect from temperatures below 50° F. (12° C.); It is best kept under lights in winter in cold-weather zones 2–7.

Blooming

These plants bloom, sporadically, in white, yellow, blue, orange, or red (according to variety); in most of the small types the bloom is a candle-shaped spear of flowers. The plant dies after blooming, hopefully having produced at least one proliferation or "pup."

DANDELION *(Taraxacum officinale)*: Most zones. Accent.

That's what we said; dandelion for accent plant! When considered seriously, it's quite logical; What blooms more beautifully, has a more interesting and lovely seedhead, and grows with such dedication as our friend the lawn buttercup, or dandelion? The Japanese have long recognized the value of this plant and devote much concern to its culture, which is more involved than one might expect. As an accent or companion plant it gives a spot of color and is used in a composition to indicate summer. A symmetrical, single-crowned plant is selected and dug—not pulled up—with all its taproot intact. Allow the leaves to wilt, then coil the root, fit it into a small, shallow pot, and carefully add soil. Try it, you'll like it!

Feeding

Feed only once or twice a year, something like 7–10–9.

Light

Give full sun.

Watering

Do not allow the plant to dry out.

DWARF BABY TEARS *(Helxine soleirolii)*: Zones 7–10, sometimes survives winter zones 5–6. Ground cover.

H. soleirolii forms a beautiful mat of tiny round leaves, and must be frequently thinned or the root system will become so extensive and growth so rampant it may compete with the trees.

Soil and watering

Likes a sandy soil and plenty of water so long as drainage is good.

Pruning

Can be cut back for greater neatness.

Location

Grows best in greenhouse conditions. Do not expose to bright sunlight.

DWARF EGYPTIAN PAPYRUS *(Cyperus):* **Zones 9–10. Accent plant.**

From a distance this plant looks like a clump of little palm trees, with smooth straight trunks and heads of grassy fronds. The head sprouts tiny plantlets from the crown. Growers propagate papyrus by pinning the severed head upside down in moist soil, which gives rise to one of its common names, "upside down plant." Some scholars believe this is the bullrush that surrounded the cradle of the baby Moses.

Watering

These are bog plants, and should either stand in water or be kept very moist.

Feeding

Feed Rapid-Gro in early spring and midsummer.

Location

A few hours of sun daily in early summer and early fall will bring about shorter, more compact growth, but watch for dry, brown leaf tips, indicating the plant needs more shade.

Repotting

It may be repotted at any time.

DWARF HORSETAIL *(Equisetum sp.):* **Zones 4–10. Accent.**

This is a tapering, round, hollow, leafless cylinder, sometimes attractively marked with red and yellow bands, which grows in neat 1½–3 inch clumps. The horsetail, which has a high silica content, is one of the "scouring rushes" used by pioneer women for cleaning pots and pans. Sometimes recommended as an edible herb, its high silica content makes this a risky suggestion; mechanical poisoning may result.

Watering

The plant needs lots of water and can stand in water with no harm done.

Location

Give it morning sun or dappled shade.

DWARF RIVER RUSH *(Eleocharis)*: **Zones 5–10. Accent.**

This plant looks like a tiny cylindrical-leaved grass, 1–2 inches (2.6–5.1 cm) high. Aquarium shops sometimes sell a taller variety as "Hair Grass." Dwarf river rush is especially pretty tucked into a corner of the lake compartment of a kawamoto water basin planting tray.

Watering

Rushes grow fairly well when completely submerged but are best as a bog plant.

Location

Give it morning sun, or dappled shade.

DWARF VIOLET *(Viola minima, V. nana compacta)*: **Zones 5–10. Bonsai accent.**

Often regarded as a weedy pest in lawns, *V. minima* and *nana* are lovely when studied at close range, as a free-blooming mass nestled in a saikei or covering the soil of a medium to large bonsai. Never exceeding one-third inch (1.3 cm), the plants will bloom outside during most of the summer and for over a month more when brought into the house and grown under lights or in a bright window.

Propagation

When old plants become straggly and stop blooming cut them off to make room for their seedlings.

Location

Give full sun or partial shade.

Watering

Keep moist but not soggy.

IVY *(Hedera helix)*: **Hardiness varies with variety. Bonsai or accent.**

For many years growers have been developing variations on a theme; find and develop the most possible kinds of shapes and colors and sizes of ivy. One of the most popular of all plants, ivy comes in a great variety of leaf colors (pink, yellow, white, and cream, as well as all shades and tints of green), leaf shapes may be large and round, heart-shaped, one-, three-, five-, or seven-lobed, pointed, or thread-like. Leaf textures may be smooth, crinkled, wavy, or wildly fluted.

It's hard to choose whether this fine plant should be in Favorite Trees (Chapter 11), or Accent Plants and Ground Covers, for it makes a beautiful tree-like specimen, and can be fairly large, but most are seen as small bonsai, ground cover, or accent (companion) plants, so we'll present it in this category.

Propagation

The quickest way to obtain a handsome specimen is to air-layer an old branch. If it is from the top of a plant as high as 15–20 feet (4.5–6 meters) (one that has perhaps climbed a tree, wall, or chimney) you can get a blooming specimen, as ivy only blooms when very tall. A plant that has reached this height will be different from one at the ground level: usually the leaves have fewer or no lobes.

Location

Some *H. helix* varieties can take full sun, but most want only morning sun or dappled to full shade. It depends upon leaf color as well as variety, so experiment if you can't find someone who can tell you.

Winter

Most are fairly hardy; here again there is quite a variation.

Soil

All take a standard soil, with some pea- and nutmeg-size gravel added. The gravel encourages more character in the trunks and branches, for as the roots encounter the obstructions and grow around them, the top of the plant develops in a stockier way.

Problems

Good house plants, but watch for mites, scales, aphids, and mealy bugs. Use a detergent bath against the insects, and shower the plant frequently.

Feeding

Feed 7–12–10 at half strength monthly during the growing season, alternating occasionally with half-strength Rapid-Gro.

Repotting

Repot once or twice yearly in the spring and late fall.

Shaping

Wiring probably will never be necessary, but you may want to stake the center leader if the plant does not shape up as you desire.

With a little patience and care, fine specimens are produced. Our favorite is *H. faerber,* a variety of Irish Lace (figs. 9–9, 10) which we started from a 2-inch (5.1 cm) cutting. Prunings from *faerber* have found homes all over the country, and it is the mother of a large ivy bed surrounding a birch tree on our terrace. This one is hardy in zones 6–10. Like most of the type, it may produce a maverick leaf not of the shape or size expected (a sport), which is always snipped off immediately.

MOSS (many species): Hardy in most zones. Ground cover.

Moss is considered the best of all ground covers as the texture is uniform, fine, and pleasing to touch and see (see fig. 9–8) so that the overall effect complements any tree. It also insulates tree roots from heat while moisture and soil are retained, and does not send down a root system that competes for moisture and nutrients. There is no point in identifying moss varieties; they are legion. If it looks and grows well, you have the right moss!

Problems

Moss is generally hardy. Its few drawbacks are that it seldom can be grown well on indoor bonsai and saikei; that it isn't always easy to find or establish; and that some locations are too sunny for it. In wet weather moss may be smothered by liverwort, an algae that forms fleshy, green scalloped plates over the soil surface. It smothers moss and, when dry weather returns the plates become a leathery, waterproof coat which should be removed before it spreads.

To move moss found in nature

Moss found growing on stone walls, between bricks, or on an otherwise bare lawn is usable, especially if it has been accustomed to some sun. Using a broad spatula remove it in thin sheets and place it on a top dressing of fine soil around your trees. Pat a little soil on the edges and nestle it firmly in place, pinning with copper staples if necessary. Keep moist and shaded until there is evidence of growth.

To grow moss

Found in small clumps, the moss should be dried, then passed through a fine sieve. Keep in a dry, cool place until ready to use. To plant it, sift the powdered moss over a fine top-dressing soil which has been firmed. Keep shaded, moist, and protected from pouring rain. Water by misting, or set the pot in water to the rim, then drain well as soon as soil is moist—a matter of a few minutes.

Aeration

When moss becomes a thick, perfect covering, it's wise to aerate it so it won't smother itself (one cause of brown rot-spots) and die. With tweezers, reach into

9-9 Ivy, *Hedera helix*, "Irish Lace," zones 5-10, 5 inches tall from soil surface to tip. Its bonsai name is "Faerber."

the moss at one inch intervals and pull out a few plants, leaving tiny holes. Repeat whenever necessary and if rot-spots do appear lift them out and change the soil under them immediately. Sprinkle a little moss spore on the area or allow it to remain open until surrounding moss covers the soil again. Since overwatering promotes or even causes this problem, it is a good idea to leave a little place at the back open so that you can see or feel the soil. You're less likely to overwater if it's convenient to check first.

Feeding

We never use dry fertilizer, as it can damage moss. Also, the dry carrying material may not dissolve, leaving unsightly particles.

Humping

If the moss begins to form humps, remove all the moss. Dry, sieve, and begin again. Ordinarily no hump problem occurs in the one or two seasons it can grow before repotting time returns. Overcrowding causes the humps.

ACCENT PLANTS AND GROUND COVERS **75**

9–10 One year later, it's been given a larger pot and already shows heavier leaf growth, which will promote a thicker trunk. Apex has been wired to bring it higher and above the trunk base. Wiring is seldom necessary with ivy.

SELAGINELLA *(Selaginella kraussiana brownii):* **Zones 7–10. Accent or ground cover.**

Like *Arenaria, Selaginella* bears the common names of Scotch Moss and Irish Moss. It is used as a component of saikei (see figs. 7–1, 2) and occasionally as a ground cover surrounding bonsai, but it is a little coarse for this purpose. The very interesting scale-like leaves creep close to the ground on running stems that root as they go, never reaching more than an inch in height.

Location

It must have some shade with fairly high humidity.

Propagation

Cuttings root readily. Culture is the same as for *Arenaria*, except that *Selaginella* likes a little more protection from sun and dry winds.

10. Fertilizers and Fertilizer Schedules

To cover all the possible types and uses of fertilizers would take all the space of this book and many volumes more. We'll just give an idea of what fertilizer is and an outline of the program we have found effective.

WHAT IS FERTILIZER?

ORGANIC FERTILIZER

Organic fertilizers, those made up of animal and plant matter, do have their place but they are not the main method of supplying nutrition to our bonsai and saikei. Use compost, bloodmeal, bonemeal, ground eggshells, and composted animal manures in the potting soil if you like, then go on to the *real* feeding, the controlled nutrition with elements you can analyze and balance according to need, season, and the age of the plant.

Most organic fertilizers supply one important value: that of making the soil more porous and thus more able to retain air and nutrient-laden water until it can be drawn up by the plant. But there is always the possibility of introducing disease, weed seeds, and pests with homemade fertilizer. Michigan peat, that fine, black stuff from the nursery supply shop, and sphagnum peat, the brown, fibrous medium sold for mulching and mixing into potting soil, will fulfill this humus need more safely and more conveniently. The argument that organic fertilizers supply the necessary fungus and bacteria to convert humus for plant use is erroneous. These will be present without any help from us. Prepared and dissolved nutrients have already reached the condition of availability, so that trees can use them immediately.

MAKEUP OF COMMERICAL FERTILIZERS

Fertilizer formulas are far more important than brand names, no matter what the advertisements may say. Formulas are delineated by three numbers separated by dashes. In the formula 7-14-6 the analysis is 7 percent nitrogen, 14 percent phosphorus, and 6 percent potassium. Because it contains all the most commonly needed elements, this is called a complete fertilizer.

Nitrogen is the most important element in the formula, it mainly encourages leaf growth, but contributes to the development of all other plant parts as well. Phosphorous assists root, flower, and fruit development. Potassium aids in the woody growth of stem and trunk and in the formulation and movement of carbohydrates. Trace elements—calcium, magnesium, sulfur, and a host of other minor ingredients—are also necessary, but in much smaller measure (hence "trace" meaning a very small amount), and are usually included in mixed commercial fertilizers.

There is no such thing as a general, all-purpose fertilizer. Each type of plant should have its own formulation; you wouldn't give an old Japanese peach 20-16-10, for soft suckers would develop, leaf growth would be exaggerated, and the shape would be ruined. A more realistic analysis for this plant would be approximately 7-6-19, or even 5-8-7.

SUGGESTED STRENGTH AND TYPE OF FEEDING.

The mixing directions on a package of fertilizer are conservative; our own experiments show that it would take from 4 to 7 times the recommended strength to cause fertilizer burn or other damage in most types of plants. However, we suggest mixing at ¼, ½, or even ¾ strength because we prefer the more even effect produced by feeding more frequently.

Time release fertilizers are a good idea, but water regulates the release of these chemicals. A long rainy period would play havoc with your feeding schedule, and the deficiency would not be apparent immediately.

Foliar feeding works with most plants, depending upon their ability to absorb through their leaves, but the effect is immediate and short in duration. We like to combine foliar with regular feeding by sprinkling a weak mixture over the entire plant as well as soaking the soil.

SOIL ANALYSIS

If the soil mixture is appropriate for the type of plant living in it, there is seldom any necessity for a soil analysis. Watch growth and color for clues, and furnish whatever the plant seems to need (see Chapter 16). One test that is valuable is the pH evaluation (of soil acidity). Kits can be bought inexpensively at nursery supply stores or ordered from seed catalogues. The pH reading should be somewhere between 6.0 (more acid) and 7.0 (normal). If the soil is too acid or alkaline the nutrients become unavailable—"locked up." To raise the pH reading, an alkaline substance such as ground limestone is gradually added in very small amounts. To reduce alkalinity, ammonium sulfate is especially effective. If the soil is being mixed in preparation for planting it can be tested and corrections made before it is used. Any pH adjustment on a growing plant should be gradual.

STANDARD DECIDUOUS TREE FEEDING SCHEDULE

As first buds show signs of swelling in spring, feed young, developing trees monthly, alternating 23–19–17 with 7–6–19, both mixed at half-strength. If there is too much leaf or stem growth, use the 7–6–19 for all subsequent feedings. Discontinue feeding in heat of summer and resume in cooler weather with one feeding of 7–6–19, then one of 0–10–6 or 4–10–3 three or four weeks before the first frosts are expected. For older deciduous trees follow the same schedule, using the 7–6–19 formula in place of the 23–19–17.

We use this plan for flowering and fruiting trees, beginning only after spring bloom is over.

EVERGREEN FEEDING SCHEDULE

AZALEA AND OTHER ACID-SOIL PLANTS

After blooming and repotting, feed 23–19–17 at half-strength monthly as soon as new growth begins. Discontinue feeding when growth hardens and slows in midsummer, then give two light feedings of the same analysis at eight, then six weeks before first frosts are expected.

Feed other broadleafed evergreens with the same formulation and by the same schedule as azaleas.

JUNIPER, CHAMAECYPARIS CRYPTOMERIA

Give 12–12–12 at half-strength monthly during the growing season. Discontinue in midsummer, then give 7–6–19 mixed at ¾ strength six weeks before first frosts are expected. Just before plants are put into winter protection 0–7–10 can be given.

PINES, SPRUCES

Do not begin feeding until new needles have fully expanded and hardened. Then give one feeding of 5-8-7. In the fall after cool weather arrives, offer one feeding of 0-7-10. Some older pines and spruces are not given supplemental feedings at all. If growth and color are satisfactory and repotting is done every two to three years the soil may be sufficient; however, we always feed younger trees and usually the older ones too.

If unable to find the exact formulations specified here, select some that are close. These readings are not so precise that approximations cannot be made. More specific instructions for individual plants are given in Chapter 11.

FEEDING OF ACCENT PLANTS AND GROUND COVER

Accent plants should be fed according to the demands of their type. They usually require more frequent feeding than bonsai trees and a more dilute mixture—say ¼ strength—every two weeks. Check a regular houseplant book for specific instructions applying to individual plants.

Ground covers must accept whatever is given their trees and usually seem to thrive well enough, which indicates that it's more important to give good general care than to worry about exactly the right proportion of food in the right place at the right time!

Never fertilize a dry plant; burn can result. The soil should be moist. All-soluble fertilizers are used throughout, mixed with tap water and sprinkled over the entire plant. Soil is soaked well.

SEASONAL FERTILIZING CHART

Type of plant	SPRING		SUMMER	FALL	
	What	*When*		*What*	*When*
Deciduous, flowering & fruit (young, developing)	Alternate monthly: 23–19–17 and 7–6–19 at ½ strength.	Start as first buds show signs of swelling (deciduous) or after blooming (flowering, fruit)	None	(1) 7–6–19 0–10–6 (2) 4–10–3 (all at ½ strength)	(1) Once, as weather begins to cool, then (2) 3 or 4 weeks before frost is expected
(older, mature)	If too much leaf and stem growth, use only 7–6–19	Monthly after blooming (for flowering types)	None	Same as above	One feeding 3 or 4 weeks before frost is expected
Azalea & other broadleaf evergreens	23–19–17, ¼ or ½ strength	Monthly when new growth begins after repotting	None after growth hardens in midsummer	23–19–17	(1) 8 Weeks before frost (2) 6 weeks before frost
Juniper, chamaecyparis, cryptomeria	12–12–12, ½ strength	Monthly during growing season	None in midsummer	(1) 7–6–19 at ¾ strength (2) 0–7–10	(1) 6 weeks before frost (2) Just before winter protection

Type of plant	SPRING		SUMMER	FALL	
	What	*When*		*What*	*When*
Pines, spruces	5–8–7	Once after new needles have hardened	None in midsummer	0–7–10	After cool weather arrives
Birch	5–10–10 at ¼ strength	Weekly	Stop mid-July	0–12–12	Sept. to Nov. 3 or 4 times, 2–3 weeks apart
Boxwood	12–12–12	Twice in spring, once more in 6 weeks	None in midsummer	0–7–10	Once in Sept.
Cotoneaster	Alternate 7–6–9 (Hyponex) and 23–19–17 (Rapid-Gro) ½ to ¾ strength	Monthly during growing season	Same as above	4–10–3 (Fertilome Root Stimulater)	6–8 weeks before frost
Quince	Feed as for deciduous				
Red Mangrove	Hyponex, ½ strength	Once, as growth begins	Once, in late summer		None

Benches can be struck and reassembled
when more shelf space is needed.
(Dunton collection. Dunton photo)

This Scotch pine, "Lochmoor," is 27
inches tall including the pot.
(Dunton collection. Dunton photo)

*Mamé. (Joel Gold Collection.
Dunton photo)*

This boxwood, "Serendipity," is 30 inches high including the pot.
(*Sandra Christophel collection. Dunton photo*)

Juniper, windswept style, 30 inches long. (*John Lowrance collection. Dunton photo*)

Sweet gum in fall color, "Hoi Tei,"
20 inches. *(Dunton collection.
Dunton photo)*

Blue juniper "Sunset," 8 inches high, including pot. *(Dunton collection. Dunton photo)*

Juniper, cascade style, 25 inches high.
(Dunton collection. Dunton photo)

Pinus sylvestris, literati style, 30 inches high.
(Joel Gold photo)

Juniper, variety *Cannaerti*, informal upright style. *(Joel Gold photo)*

Japanese maple "Full Moon," 21 inches. *(Ann Pipe collection. Dunton photo)*

Cotoneaster, 15 inches. (*Ann Pipe collection. Dunton photo*)

Bamboo, 16 inches, accessorized by
a very old Chinese toy.
(Ann Pipe collection. Dunton photo)

Jasmine. This particular species has a very long flowering season.
(Ann Pipe collection. Dunton photo)

Cryptomeria japonica, 28 inches high. An excellent subject for indoor culture, providing it has good strong light. Good for fluorescent light gardening. *(Joel Gold photo)*

Boxwood (*B. microphylla*, var. "Kingsville") 10 inches high. Good for indoor culture (same as *C. japonica*). (*Joel Gold photo*)

Ficus carica, 18 inches, 7 inches. *(Ann Pipe collection. Dunton photo)*

This tray of Alpine strawberries makes a unique dinner-party centerpiece.
The base is an ornate mirror. *(Dunton collection)*

Winged elm, fall color.
(Dunton collection.
Dunton photo)

Azelea Hinodegiri in spring bloom, 15 inches tall. *(Dunton collection. Dunton photo)*

Type of plant	SPRING		SUMMER	FALL	
	What	*When*	*What*	*What*	*When*
Rose	5–10–7, ½ strength	Beginning as buds start swelling, at 2 week intervals	Discontinue in heat of summer	Resume schedule, same food	2 or 3 feedings as weather cools; stop 6 weeks before frosts are expected
Serissa	Feed as for Natal Plum (Carissa)				
Texas Ebony	12–12–12, ½ strength	Every three weeks, beginning when buds loosen	None	12–12–12	Once, as temperature moderates
Willow	Feed as for deciduous				
Wisteria	5–10–10, ½ strength	Monthly, beginning as buds loosen	None in hottest part of summer	(1) 5–10–10, ½ strength (2) 0–7–10, ½ strength	(1) As temperature moderates (2) 3 weeks later

11. Favorite Trees for Bonsai

Many hundreds of kinds of trees are considered standards for bonsai use. As for new possibilities, they are limitless. Both recognized standards and some not usually considered for bonsai are included in the following list. Their elegibility is evaluated drawing upon our own experience. Your experience could contradict our findings; you might create a lovely specimen of a type we feel is not at all appropriate. If you admire the mature tree in nature, consider how well it might be miniaturized.

CRITERIA FOR BONSAI

The most likely candidates would have small leaves, twiggy growth, short stem lengths between leaf buds, and fibrous root systems (as opposed to a few heavy, long roots).

You can get a fair idea of the root pattern from the top. Trees with a single leader and sparse branches tend to have a long, heavy taproot with a few other large roots. Some of these can be trained by gradually reducing the taproot and side roots, encouraging the feeder roots to form closer and closer to the trunk as pruning is repeated each season. Some trees cannot adjust to this root pruning and may finally die, or refuse to grow well. Oak, beech, and sweetgum fall into this group. We have nice examples of all of these, but they require special treatment and are not as quickly rewarding as many other deciduous trees. Our list emphasizes deciduous trees for they grow and respond to training much faster than others and are gratifying subjects for beginner and master alike.

Trees that tend to grow many leader branches (elm, maple, most junipers, and some pines) will have a like root system, and their fibrous roots make them easier to deal with.

Trees with compound leaves (ash, locust, hickory) present an obvious complication: the long-stemmed leaves stand out and will not make well-shaped clumps near the branches. They can be cut back to the first two leaflets, but this gives them an unnatural, crippled look.

CARE OF BONSAI

The majority of the trees mentioned in the following list respond well to standard watering methods and soil mix as prescribed below. If a tree needs a special watering schedule or soil mix we will specify.

Standard watering: Water when soil begins to look dry at the surface. Soak well. Do not allow the soil to get either bone dry or soggy.

Standard soil mix: One part sand (sharp sand from the lumber yard or nursery, *not* from the sea shore, or Turface, which is a sand substitute from the nursery), one part milled brown sphagnum, and one part garden loam which has proven itself by promoting good growth in flowers, vegetables, and weeds.

The United States Department of Agriculture Hardiness Zone Map (Chapter 15) will show the accepted hardiness rating, which can vary somewhat according to micro-climate and your individual maintenance and protection methods. Sometimes the low-temperature tolerance is less important to a plant's survival than other factors, such as summer heat, wind, natural rainfall, sea-level preference, and a host of considerations. Learn as much as you can about your favorite trees, and duplicate their native habitats as far as is practical.

For map and other information on zones referred to in listings, see Chapter 15.

AZALEA *(Rhododendron sp.):* Hardiness varies with species. Any style.
The range of azaleas available to bonsai growers staggers the imagination. Azaleas, which are relatively easy to grow, give flowers, fine form, and many offer a fine fall display of colored leaves.

Repotting
Repot as soon as blooming is finished in spring. The root system is densely packed with fine hairlike roots and may become so solid in one growing season that the plant is in danger of strangling itself in the confines of a pot.

Even a young three- to four-year-old nursery plant will show a few large surface roots. Save the best ones, arrange them in the pot so they don't overlap, and train them early—in a few seasons they will be too rigid to train.

At each repotting comb out the tangled roots, trim them off, then take out several pie-shaped sections (see fig. 12–19) to leave room in the root ball for new development. Work around the surface roots, leaving them undisturbed. This method is useful for any densely rooted tree.

Shaping

Prune branches before beginning to repot. Cut off all seed pods left by the flowers—they draw too much strength from the rest of the plant and give it a frowsy appearance. Thin out the fine twigs, leaving one or two to each cluster, and remove whole clusters where the branching is too dense. If the leaf-mass seems to be getting too far from the main branch, you may cut back all the twigs. Azaleas can be cut back drastically and will develop buds all along a branch or trunk. Wiring can be done at any time, but remember that mature wood is very brittle and snaps if not manipulated gently and gradually. Trunk and branch expansion is rapid so the wire must be removed in a few weeks—watch them closely.

Location

Azaleas prefer dappled shade all day or morning sun with afternoon shade.

Watering

They should never dry out. Since the soil contains so much peat it may look dark and wet even when it is dry. Check carefully, for these plants use a lot of water and dry out more quickly than might be expected.

Soil

A good soil mixture is three parts black Michigan peat, one part sand or Turface, and one part garden loam. Good results are also found using only peat, but we feel the above mix gives the best growth and bloom.

Feeding

Feed Rapid-Gro at ¼ or ½ strength once monthly as soon as new growth is evident after repotting. Discontinue feeding when growth hardens and slows in hottest weather. One or two light ¾ strength feedings may be given at eight and six weeks before first frosts are to be expected in your area (see chart in Chapter 10).

If leaves look yellow or have a reddish mottling, add one teaspoon of white vinegar to every quart of water at every watering for a week or two. (See Chapter 15 for testing and adjusting pH of water.)

Winter care

Learn the hardiness zone of each type you want, and give appropriate winter protection (see Chapter 15).

BEECH *(Fagus):* **Zones 4–8. Groves, informal and formal upright.**

A good subject, despite the long taproot, not-so-generous branching, and rather sparse twigs. The trunk becomes a smooth light gray with age, and the leaves and leaf-buds are handsome. The growth habit is shelf-like, the branches arranging themselves in strata, in all but the narrow upright types *(excelsia stricta)*.

Shaping

Seldom needs wiring. Leaf prune as soon as first leaves harden, no later. This tree has one budding season, spanning April, May, and June, and leaves pruned after this time won't be replaced. This is one of the deciduous trees that many growers do not leaf prune, but we recommend it as the results are worthwhile. Be careful not to injure the leaf-buds since they extend past the stem bases of the existing leaves. Do not leaf prune every year. Growth is fairly rapid from infancy to adolescence, and it makes a very distinguished looking tree, even in adolescence.

Location

Morning sun only, or dappled sun.

Watering

Water as soil begins to look dry. Do not allow to dry out.

Feeding

Follow the standard deciduous fertilizing program.

Soil

1–1–1 soil mix.

BIRCH *(Betula):* **Zones 3–8. Groves, informal upright.**

There are dwarf alpine birches which are interesting for *mamé* or terrains. Our favorite is *Betula nigra,* black river birch, which is relatively large, easy to transplant from the wild, and makes a lovely grove if carefully pinched and de-suckered. (Old trained trees die if suckers are permitted to grow out from the roots or low on the trunk. Remove these immediately.)

Repotting

Do this in spring as buds swell. We have successfully collected young, 15–18 inch (38–46 cm) seedlings, leafed out and bare root, in July, but we would never attempt to move an old tree at this time.

Problems

Birches are subject to leaf miners, borers, caterpillars, and aphids (which carry a leaf distorting blight). Spray with Isotox or other systemic.

Location

Give dappled sun.

Feeding

Feed 5–10–10 ¼ strength weekly, from early spring to July 15. Resume with 0–12–12 from September to November, giving three or four feedings two or three weeks apart.

Soil

Add one part sand and pea gravel to the standard soil mix.

Watering

In midsummer, stand pot or tray in shallow water. Never allow it to dry out. Sprinkle leaves frequently.

BOXWOOD *(Buxus sp.):* **Zones of hardiness vary. Any style except cascade.**

There are many species of boxwood, most of them splendid for bonsai (figs. 11–1, 2, 3). They tend to have small evergreen leaves, with a polished, very neat appearance. The bark becomes furrowed at an early age, and fine *mamé* can be developed in a short time, even though the plant is slow-growing. Larger specimens can be pruned down from nursery stock, and if you make a lucky find you'll immediately have a handsome specimen to train and perfect for all the years to come—it's a long-lived tree.

Feeding

Give 12–12–12 twice in spring, beginning as soon as the new leaves have expanded, then again six weeks later. In about September, give one fall feeding of 0–7–10 or something similar. Offer no nitrogen in the fall or there will be winter-kill of new soft branches.

Location

Boxwood likes full sun or dappled sun. Protect leaves and bark from winter sunshine.

Shaping

Never leaf prune, but branches may be pruned and shaped at any time. Wires may not be necessary, but if they are used, be careful; the old wood is brittle and the younger bark is soft and marks easily.

11-1 Old boxwood "Serendipity," 20 inches. (*Christophel collection*)

11-2 Detail showing bark texture.

11-3 Small leaves make most boxwoods good subjects.

Watering

Do not allow to dry out—water when soil begins to look dry.

COTONEASTER *(Cotoneaster—*say "koe toe nee aster"**): Zones vary. Any style.**

This is an obliging plant which offers many fine features for bonsai culture: small pink flowers and round red fruit on ultra-short stems, small leaves (except for a very few types), a tolerance for small pots and heavy pruning. They are pretty even as very young specimens (fig. 11–4).

The rockspray types (zones 5–9) are well named; their branches spray out in a fishbone pattern at horizontal or drooping angles.

C. microphylla thymifolia (zones 8–9) has leaves very much like its namesake thyme and tiny pale pink flowers the size of half a pea. The ovoid fruit is red and slightly larger.

Feeding

Feed monthly during the growing season, alternating 7–6–19 (Hyponex) and 23–19–17 (Rapid-Gro). Mix at ½ to ¾ strength. Discontinue in heat of summer, then give 4–10–3 (Fertilome Root Stimulator) six to eight weeks before first frosts may be expected in your area.

Location

Give morning sun and afternoon shade. Does very well under light, but watch for spider mites. Mites of all kinds proliferate in light gardens, where there is no rain or dew.

Water

Mist daily (see Chapter 15, General Care, Fluorescent Light Gardening). Do not allow to dry out; water when soil looks dry at surface.

CRAPE MYRTLE *(Lagerstroemia indica):* **Freezes to the ground in zones 5–6, hardy 7–8. Multistemmed or informal upright.**

Crape myrtle has pink, white, lavender, or red flowers, a slightly weeping habit, and tends to bloom when small. Remove old blossoms promptly. Good as a multistemmed plant, or it can be trained to a single-trunk informal upright style.

There are dwarf crape myrtles, which bloom at a very small size. The flowers are charming—like crinkled bits of silk crepe. Bloom is from midsummer to frost.

Location

Give it full sun.

11-4 Even very young cotoneasters bloom well, with flowers in perfect scale.

Water
   Standard watering.

Soil
   Standard soil mix.

Feeding
   Feed 12–12–12 when growth begins in spring, then feed monthly 8–10–4 (this analysis can be found in rose food) at half-strength until six weeks before first frost is expected.

Winter protection

To preserve the trunk the plant must be allowed to go dormant, then wintered over in a cold-frame or (in zones 5–6) a cold room where temperatures will remain above freezing. In zones 7–8, mulch to first branches at the first sign of cold weather.

Repotting

Repot in October or November, whenever leaves fall and dormancy begins.

Shaping

Do not wire, for the branches are very brittle. Crape myrtle blooms in mid-summer, so pinch new growth twice to encourage branching (during the first four weeks of growth) then cut back to shape after bloom is over.

ELM *(Ulmus):* **Hardiness varies with species. Groves, formal and informal upright, slanting, windblown sinuous, broom.**

The elms offer some of the very best possibilities (figs. 11–5, 6). The leaves of most species dwarf very well, even the large-leaved American elm *(Ulmus americana)*; however, because of its susceptibility to several serious diseases, we don't use the American elm.

Feeding

Use the standard deciduous feeding schedule (Chapter 10).

JAPANESE GREYBARK ELM

This famous elm *(U. zelkova)* is often trained in the broom style, but it also makes a very stately formal or informal upright. New leaves are red and mature to green. Hardy zones 3–8.

CHINESE ELM

U. parvifolia is a popular bonsai subject for good reason (figs. 11–7, 8). We know of no other tree that can go from matchstick seedling to handsome bonsai in such a short time. Chinese elm is presentable in three years—impressive in

11-5 Elm leaves—left *Hokaido*, middle a bonsai Chinese elm, right, leaves taken from a Chinese elm planted as a lawn tree, a brother to the bonsai Chinese elm. They are all the same age. Scissors are 7 inches long.

11-6 Winged elm collected 15 years ago, 18 inches high. *(Dunton collection)*

five! It makes an excellent *mamé* and all other sizes are of like quality. It can be had from most nurseries as hedging plants.

Fastest development of the Chinese elm takes place when planted in a bed (this tree can shoot up 6 feet (1.7 meters) in one summer) but then almost daily attention is necessary during the growing season. Growth is slower but easier to control if trees are planted in large, low pots sunk in soil just above the rims. They *must* be repotted every spring.

Roots can and should be cut back by half at the first planting, and the tap root can be cut all the way off if there are other feeder roots. Be meticulous about spreading and arranging roots; they tangle if left to themselves.

A fine beginner's tree and a credit to the advanced grower, for all the desired potential is there, needing only attention and discipline. Very hardy, zones 3–8. (This is not recommended, but one midwest grower of our acquaintance leaves his Chinese elms outside on the bench all winter.)

EVERGREEN ELM

U. parvifolia sempervirens grows in zones 6–8 in any style except for cascade. There is an improved *sempervirens* called catlin. This is slower growing than the Chinese elm with even smaller leaves, which are dark and glossy. It has such long sturdy roots that it adapts easily to the root-over-rock style. An excellent subject, it can be kept in a sunny window or under plant lights all winter then repotted in spring; there is no need to worry about repotting it while it is in full leaf. Kept outside in winter, it becomes dormant, with the leaves hanging on until new buds push them off. Feed as for any deciduous, but if long, awkward-looking branches develop, cut back on feeding.

HOKKAIDO

There is an even smaller-leaved elm, the Hokkaido (see fig. 11–5), from the Hokkaido prefecture in Japan. It is hardy, growing in zones 7–9, and has the smallest imaginable leaves, somewhat like juniper scales. Train and maintain as for catlin, above.

EUONYMOUS: Hardy zones 4–8.
There are hundreds of species of euonymous, ranging from vine to shrub to tree, and many are eligible for bonsai. *Euonymous alata compacta altropurpea* is a fine subject. The bark acquires character in three or four years and the deep red fall color is dazzling. The word *alatus* tells us the branches have corky

11-7 Chinese elm being pruned to shape, 6 inches.

11-8 Small bonsai, all under 6 inches. *(Dunton collection)*

wings, an interesting feature. The tiny greenish flowers, plentiful and well in scale, mature into three-lobed brilliant pink and orange fruits in late summer and fall.

Soil

Use the standard mix (one part peat, one part garden loam, one part sand).

Feeding

E. compacta is such a heavy feeder that its leaves will become blotched and reddish if not fed generously. Give a ¼ strength feeding every two weeks of 12–12–12 from April 15 to July 15 (zones 4–7), resuming in early September with 0–12–12 at ⅓ strength every two weeks until October 15.

Watering

Do not allow complete drying out. Give lots of water.

Repotting

Repot in spring as buds swell. The fibrous root system is so dense that it repels water once it gets really dry. The cut-pie section method, as described for azaleas, must be used at every repotting.

Shaping

Wiring is usually not necessary, but if it is done, use either paper-wrapped wires or weights. Branches may tend to form too-narrow forks; prop them apart with sticks. Trunk and branches increase rather rapidly; check wiring frequently. There is one budding season per year, so do not leaf-prune.

Location

If the tree is in a large, deep pot full sun will be best, but in any shallow bonsai pot afternoon shading is recommended as transpiration is so rapid that there is danger of drying out.

Problems

Euonymous is subject to scale; use Isotox in a regular spray program.

Fig (Ficus): Zones 8–9. Varied styles, especially groves.

The Ficus family, with over 500 species, contains some of the prettiest, least demanding species available to the Southern landscape, to the house-plant enthusiast, and to the bonsai grower (figs. 11–9, 10).

Of the same family as the banyan, in which a single tree develops into a whole grove, F. benjamina, F. benjamina exotica and F. nerifolia (willow-leaf fig) also can be encouraged to develop the adventitious roots from trunk and

11-9 *Ficus benjamina* grove, 20 inches high. Obvious pruning scar at apex on left tree will disappear in time, but should be painted for concealment. (*Ralph Young collection*)

11-10 Roots of *F. benjamina* showing banyan-like tendencies.

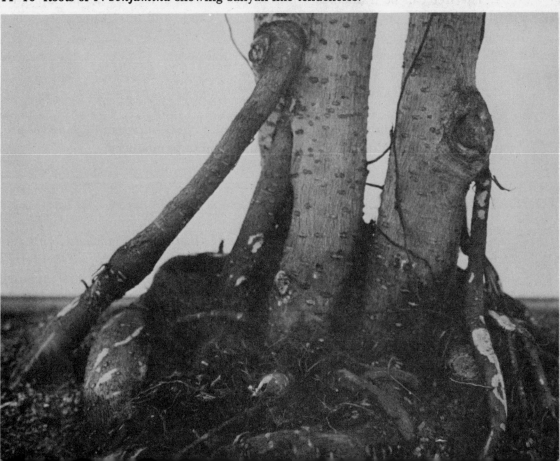

lower limbs which bring about this phenomenon. A well-grown *Ficus* in a humid atmosphere sends down roots from the trunk and lower horizontal limbs. They touch the ground and take hold, continuing the process until a series of trees, all interrelated, are formed. The fruit is a small, round berry in good scale and decorative for bonsai trees but a serious problem in landscape specimens. It's very attractive to birds, making a seasonal mess of dropping, rotting fruit and overactive birds.

F. BENJAMINA

The mature tree can be seen in southern parts of Florida, Arizona, California, and Texas. Used as a landscape plant they are beautiful, becoming huge shade trees covering entire lots if left untended or they can be restricted to any reasonable size by pruning. The leaves are ½ inch wide and 2½ to 3½ inches in length—a long graceful oval tapering to a slender, curving point. Older leaves are deep, shiny green; younger leaves first appear in light chartreuse, gradually darkening as they age. In a hospitable environment each leaf lives several years. In a pot the leaves dwarf by about ⅓ to ½—not really small enough but still a good subject for bonsai.

The twigs are supple, drooping slightly. At all ages the bark is fine textured, smooth, and gray with narrow darker gray horizontal striations. A young or adolescent tree has a round trunk and branches which become irregular, looking as if great muscles ran the length of them as it matures.

Surface roots develop early, radiating in a regular wheel pattern. As the years pass the roots become much taller in profile, standing ridged and sturdy as if designed by a structural engineer to support the enormous spread.

The tree can be trained as a tall narrow formal upright, informal upright, slanting trunk, or grove style. Its best, most exotic and intriguing style is the single-tree grove!

F. BENJAMINA EXOTICA

This tree is slightly more graceful than the *F. benjamina* and the leaves are narrower and smaller. The weeping habit is more pronounced.

F. NERIFOLIA

This willow-leaf fig is a more refined tree than the *benjamina*s, with the foregoing characteristics present in smaller scale. The leaves are 1 to 1½ inches long, and ⅓ of an inch or less wide, curling as they first appear, growing to a narrow, gentle curve. They are especially desirable for bonsai cultivation. It requires the same care as the *benjamina*s.

F. PUMILA

A tiny leaved climber (see fig. 9–4). Given warmth, high humidity, and strong light, it will form a ground cover or climb a wall or tree trunk, hugging its support with each leaf. It can be pruned to *mamé* specifications also. Soil, feeding, and exposure are the same as for the other *Ficus* plants except that full sun is not advised. Occasionally *F. pumila* will send out a branch with leaves that look more like those of the *benjamina* than its own. These are seed-producing branches. They seldom fruit.

Soil

In nature *Ficus* plants are generally found growing and thriving in little more than dirty sand, but this is a dangerous mix for bonsai as it dries out too fast. Good growth is produced in a mix of ½ sand, ¼ peat or compost, ¼ good loam. Turface or other clay particles can be substituted for sand, but internodes will be shorter and branching more dense if a medium fine, sharp sand is used. Good drainage is essential.

Watering

The tree must never go bone dry. If it does, the inner leaves will be shed and replaced only partially when proper watering is resumed. Complete defoliation may take place with partial or full recovery.

The wick method of watering (see Chapter 15) can be used if watering can't be attended to regularly. However, constant wicking will cause much longer internodes, a natural tendency of the *Ficus* which we should curtail as much as possible for best appearance and to keep it in scale.

Location

In homes and commercial buildings, where *benjamina* and *exotica* are immensely popular, a wide range of light intensity is tolerated by them, from the dim light where philodendron, sanseveria, and Swedish ivy will barely survive to full sun. This is not to advise the concentrated heat and light of a blazing south bay window for the tree, but it is unusually adaptable.

Ficus can be put outside in cool-weather zones as soon as the nighttime temperatures can be trusted to remain above 50 degrees F. Watch carefully for leaf-burn (brown dry blotches on the pale green, newer leaves). Start them outside in dappled or full shade, moving them gradually into stronger light. In midsummer, when light is strongest or when there is unusual sunspot activity (as in the summer of '77), move to dappled shade.

Problems

Mealy bugs, spider mites, and scale are common pests, proliferating when the air is dry. Frequent Palmolive showers, followed by thorough rinsing, can cure or even prevent pest damage on *Ficus* plants. Cover soil with plastic wrap during treatment of large plants and hold small trees on their sides over the sink. If the invaders are persistent, give the soil surface a light treatment as well, always rinsing afterwards.

TO DEVELOP THE TYPICAL BANYAN GROVE STYLE

Ideally, a tree grown in a humid atmosphere will spontaneously develop air roots from the lower trunk and bottom side of the lowest horizontal branches. If this happens, do not touch the developing nodules on trunk or branches. But as we know, most conditions are not ideal. A more reliable method is to train the lower branches horizontally with wire, weights, or tie-downs, and defoliate selected side branches, which are tip-pruned, dipped in root hormone, bent straight down, buried, and fastened securely. Try not to move the tree until the branches are well rooted as any disturbance may injure the delicate new roots, possibly killing them. Do not initiate this training until the trunk is a good size; the trunk increase will be very slow after the branches root.

If you have a tree you especially like that has no long sideshoots on the proper branches, you may use the branch-tips themselves for rooting. Another method is to make hardware-cloth cylinders, nick the branch underside, apply root hormone, place a sphagnum-packed cylinder under each nick so that the nick touches the sphagnum, and secure it with rubber bands. Keep the cylinders damp, using the drip method or frequent sprinkling. Do not over-water the roots of the tree. This usually works but is very slow and doesn't take 100 percent of the time. Most often many roots develop where you wanted just one or two. As soon as the roots begin to increase in size carefully start to remove the top part of the packing, encouraging the roots to continue down to the soil. Select the strongest roots, cutting away the smaller ones.

Ficus and many other trees can be branch-grafted in the fashion of English apple tree arbors, in which trees are planted close together, same-size branches are cut diagonally, bound together with rubber bands or tape, and covered at the jointing with grafting wax. Be sure to match cambium layers carefully.

TO OBTAIN A SHORT, BROAD-TRUNKED SPECIMEN

For this style you will reduce the crown and raise the roots. Select the level on the trunk where you want roots, and gouge out 3 to 7 places around the trunk where you want roots to form. Make a long enough cut to turn the resulting strip outward. Use a carving gouge or a very sharp knife. Brush with root hormone under each cut section. Roll a ball of clay in root hormone, and wedge the strips out at an angle. The cut should go through the cambium layer.

Root prune ¼ to ⅓ of the existing roots and plant in a deep pot, using 3 parts sand, 1 part peat, 1 part loam. Water with Transplantone or some other transplanting compound in a weak solution. Keep in shade and watch for new growth on the pruned crown, then begin to ease the tree into more sunlight until three or four hours of full sun are received without any browning of leaves. Keep moist but do not overwater. Mist foliage frequently when sun is not on the leaves.

When new roots develop in 12-14 months, cut off the lower ones, shortening the tree from the bottom, or you can gradually remove the soil, exposing some impressive aerial roots. With this method, you may want to treat the lower branches also, making roots extending from branch to ground.

TO DEVELOP A HEAVILY BUTTRESSED TRUNK

Here is yet another way of getting an authentic-looking banyan: Split a large (up to 1 inch) cutting ⅓ or more of the way up into 3 to 5 sections. Roll balls of moist clay coated in root hormone, and pack into spaces to hold the sections apart. Place cutting in a mix of 2 parts fairly coarse sand, 2 parts perlite, 1 part black peat, using enough mix to barely cover splits. The bottom half of the rooting medium should be coarse sand—brown aquarium gravel is good. As roots appear and begin to thicken gradually remove topsoil to reveal a stilted banyan. Roots will finally unite, making a solid buttress.

This process—from cutting to growing tree—takes from 18 months to 2 years. Watch for new leaf growth which indicates roots have begun to function. Give ¼ strength 5–7–12 with every second or third watering. When roots are growing well, repot in soil mixture recommended for growing *Ficus*.

Shaping
The natural shape of a mature *Ficus* is a very broad, flat umbrella (see figs. 19-1, 2). There is little if any apex. The tops have a tendency to yield vitality to the side branches and often die themselves. Prevent this by keeping the side branches nipped back. The top must also be nipped but growth can be evened by paying close attention to side branches. If a branch above your chosen primary branches begins to enlarge too much, defoliate it once yearly to slow its progress.

There is no need to use a sealing compound on pruning cuts; in fact, some say coal-tar tree sealer is harmful to *Ficus*. If pruning is done in full sun the latex sap from the tree will harden and seal the cuts even faster.

Feeding

During spring and late summer, feed ½ strength Rapid-Gro every two weeks or ¼ strength weekly. Omit feeding in winter and midsummer.

Repotting

This may be done at any time but the preferred repotting time would be late spring, just before the tree begins to respond to increased light and heat. Always shade well for two weeks after repotting and never bare the roots completely.

Watering

Mist leaves frequently but do not overwater, giving water only when soil begins to dry at the surface.

Propagation

Figs root easily from cuttings and don't really need rooting hormone. Seedlings develop into the best specimens but be sure snails and slugs cannot reach the young trees; they will decimate them quickly.

Location

Figs brought in for the winter will drop as much as one-third of their leaves, since there won't be enough sunshine to support the leaf mass built up outdoors during the summer. This can be partially obviated by pruning at the time they are moved indoors. (This advice applies to many other tropicals as well; carissa, serissa, boxwood, ivy, and Catlin elm, among others.)

Besides the varieties already mentioned, *Ficus eugeniodes, F. hillii, F. columelaris* (leaves are not as small, but it readily produces aerial roots), *F. rubiginosa, F. milcrocarpa, F. superba, F. obliqua,* are also good bonsai possibilities. All these plants are easy subjects. Such a malleable, cooperative plant family as the *Ficus* deserves the best possible management so that it can offer its finest performance.

HACKBERRY *(Celtis)*: **Zones vary. Grove, informal and formal upright.**

There is a hackberry or its close relative for every climate zone save the northernmost ones. This is lucky for it can be an impressive bonsai. The leaves dwarf well and the fruit is small and in good scale.

C. occidentalis is native to zones 3–6. It develops a gray, warty bark while still young that is very interesting and distinctive. Fruit is small and purple.

C. laevigata, C. tenuifolia, C. linkheimerii, and *C. reticulata* are native to zones 5–10 (southeast half), and all are equally suited to our use. These varieties, which are often called sugarberries, are especially twiggy, making a delicate, lacy appearance in winter. Fruits vary from yellow to orange to red, according to species, and are well liked by birds. A close relative, *Trema micrantha,* which is evergreen, is found in Florida.

Repotting

All species, including the evergreen type, should be repotted in spring as soon as buds begin to swell. Look for the buds at the bases of the old leaves.

Shaping

Wiring is seldom necessary. The twigs and branches quickly harden into horizontal angles that are appropriate to bonsai with little encouragement.

Feeding

Fertilize as for any deciduous.

Location

Place in full sun.

HAWTHORNE *(Crataegus):* **Various zones. Any style except cascade.**

All of the many varieties of hawthorne are valuable as bonsai, for the leaves are small and can dwarf even further, the flowers and fruit are in good scale, and the form is very pleasing. Problems of rusts and other diseases are always present so be prepared to follow a regular spraying schedule if you want this one to be at its best. Times for treatment vary widely from one area to another, as do the types of diseases and pests, so seek the advice of your county agent (U.S. Department of Agriculture).

BLACK HAWTHORN

In nature, *C. douglasii* grows only in the extreme northwest but it can survive zones 6–8 with protection. Leaves are broad, irregularly serrated ovals, about 1–2 inches (2.6–5.1 cm) long. Fruits are blackish and pea sized. The white, fragrant flowers appear in clusters.

DOWNY HAWTHORNE

The *C. mollis* thrives in zones 3–6. It has broad, ragged, heart-shaped leaves about 3 inches (7.6 cm) long which dwarf well. It tends to bloom when fairly young, producing clusters of many small white flowers. The fruit is a rose-red color and is especially pretty with the distinctive apple taste that is characteristic of the family.

LITTLEHIP HAWTHORNE

This hawthorne *(C. spathulata),* which grows in zones 6–9, has especially pretty, tiny, fruits and flowers. The leaves, which have the typical three-lobed shape of the popular Washington hawthorne, are only one inch (2.6 cm) long.

Our native hawthornes, as well as the introduced ones, are in such good scale for our purpose they should not be overlooked. Find them in deciduous woods, along roadsides, or even in flowerbeds or along gravel walks.

Propagation
Hawthornes can be easily air-layered, but the best specimens are developed from seedlings. Most produce suckers from far-spreading roots which can easily be moved in spring when there is very little root system.

Watering
Keep moist, watering when the soil surface begins to look dry.

Location
Tolerates any exposure, but best growth is produced in morning sun and afternoon shade.

Soil
Use a standard 1–1–1 soil mix.

Feeding
Follow the schedule described for deciduous flowering trees (see Chapter 10).

HINOKI CYPRESS *(Chamaecyparis obtusa nana):* Zones 6–9. Any style.
Chamaecyparis looks a great deal like juniper, but with finer-textured foilage (fig. 11–11).

Shaping
It is pruned in the same fashion as a juniper, expect that not all the new growth should be cut off as it will not regenerate on old growth (as will a juniper). For this reason new buds must be faithfully pruned off during the summer. Allow only one bud-length of growth before pruning new buds again.

Care
See the section on junipers for directions on care.

11-11 *Mamé chamyciperous* 3 inches high. (*Joel Gold collection. Cleo Stephens, photo*)

JAPANESE CEDAR, BANDAI SUGI *(Cryptomeria,* many species): **Zones 5–8. Any style except cascade.**

In Japan, *Cryptomeria* is a huge timber tree with shaggy reddish bark. It makes an excellent bonsai, especially for indoors. If enough strong light is provided, *Cryptomeria* can become a permanent resident on the coffee table or in a fluorescent light garden (see fig. 7-1). It looks a little like our junipers, but the needles are pointed rather than scale-like and they have a waxy shine.

Shaping

Pruning techniques are the same as for junipers. Pinch only new growth at branch tips or remove whole twigs or branches. In pruning, remember that new growth seldom develops on old wood where there are no visible buds.

Feeding

Fertilize as for junipers. If plants are kept indoors under lights feed as for early summer. The lights demand response from the trees and will deplete their strength if fertilizer is not given.

Watering

Mist often to prevent a mite invasion! Standard evergreen watering.

Location

Give full sun until summer heat begins then move to a location where the plants will receive morning sun and afternoon shade or dappled sun.

Repotting

Repot in the spring.

JASMINE *(Jasminum):* **Zones 9-10. Cascade, semicascade.**

These lovely plants are really vines but they can be trained into a graceful weeping tree. The leaves are waxy; the white or yellow flowers are gardenia-fragrant and bloom over a long period starting in early spring (see fig. 11-12).

Location

Dappled shade is best; protect from temperatures below 40° F. (7° C.).

Repotting

This should be done at the beginning of the growing season when buds begin to swell at leaf axils.

Feeding

During the growing season give ½ strength Rapid-Gro or azalea food every 4

11–12 Jasmine, 14 inches. *(Ann Pipe collection)*

weeks. If leaves begin to yellow, give a liquid feeding and spraying or chelated iron. Reddish leaves indicate soil may be too alkaline so water with acidulated water (2 teaspoons white vinegar to one quart water) once or twice.

Problems

Jasmine plants are subject to mealy bugs.

JUNIPERS *(Juniperus sp.):* **Zones 4–8, some to 9 and 10. Any style.**

Here in Missouri we always called junipers "cedars," but this is inaccurate for the only true cedars are the *Cedrus* family—*atlas, lebonii*—native to southern Europe and Asia.

Junipers are among the easiest and most rewarding subjects for bonsai. Most of them are very hardy, and they can be trained to any shape and size. The tiny scale-like leaves become bunchy and mosslike in appearance as they mature, the bark exfoliates even in young trees, and surface roots develop (see figs. 11–13, 14, 15, 16, 17, 18).

Shaping

To make growth clumpy, luxuriant, and shapely, hold the branch with one hand and pick off all the new growth at the tips (see fig. 3–10). The new buds tend to be fatter and rounder than the older leaves so it is easy to feel which

11–13 A rock-planted *Shimpaku*, (*Juniperus chinensis* "Shimpaku") tree, 8 inches. (*Joel Gold collection. Cleo Stephens, photo*)

11–14 A dramatic and very old juniper, 30 inches long. (*John Lowrance collection*)

11–15 Cascade juniper, 20 inches. (*Dunton collection*)

11-16 Cascade juniper, 27 inches. (*Dunton collection*)

11-17 This cascade has more than one good side.

11-18 *Mamé* cascade juniper less than 3 inches. (*Joel Gold collection. Cleo Stephens, photo*)

ones should be picked off. Allow some time for branching growth then repeat the process when the branches begin to look unkempt. This must be done several times in a summer and is a wearisome job when a large tree is involved. Resist the temptation to use scissors on the buds, as this ruins the looks of the tree—each cut scale turns brown and looks withered and ragged. Scissors are perfectly all right though to remove a twig or branch. Juniper branches can be pruned back as far as green growth can be seen and will grow out again, but do not expect brown branches to bud.

The fine, fibrous juniper roots can be pruned back more than other evergreens as they regenerate quickly. If enough top is removed at repotting time (half the leaf and branch mass or close to it) the root ball may be reduced by half.

Location

Give them full sun in an airy position.

Feeding

During the growing season feed 12–12–12 at ½ strength monthly. Discontinue in midsummer then resume with 7–6–19 mixed at ¾ strength in late August and late September.

Some very fine native junipers have been collected and adapted for bonsai in the western part of the United States. The east and southeast also have contributed generously, for this tree is not difficult to transplant from the wild if reasonable care is observed.

Soil

Use standard soil mix but add another part of sand and a cup of bonemeal to each half bushel of soil mix.

Types

Landscaping and bonsai nurseries offer a good variety of juniper types, all of which are rewarding candidates for "Instant Bonsai" (Chapter 5). A mature *procumbens* plant, for instance, looks lovely as soon as it is pruned and potted. It will, of course, continue to improve from that point on. *J. chinensis* "Shimpaku," the famous Sargent's juniper, is one of the better types to search for, as are the *J. chinensis* "Blawii," *J. chinensis* "Torulosa" or "Hollywood," lovely waxy scales, not too prickly, *J. procumbens nana*, one of the many *procumbens* types which is adaptable to nearly any style and size.

MAPLES *(Acer sp.):* Zones vary with variety. Root-over rock, grove, formal and informal upright, multi-trunk.

Here is another bonsai standard which offers infinite variety in form, leaf

11-19 Full moon maple, 18 inches. (*Ann Pipe collection*)

size, color, and shape. There is a maple of some kind for every zone (fig. 11–19).

Possibly the most widespread is the red maple *(Acer rubrum)*, which is native to the eastern half of the country. It makes a good bonsai in a short time and even though it is considered a short-lived tree as maples go, it can survive for fifty to sixty years. The leaves dwarf beautifully and in the fall turn shades of red mixed sometimes with a little yellow. In spring the smooth, light gray bark is a pretty background for the red flower clusters. Surface roots develop in a few years.

Another good subject, especially for Floridians, is the Florida maple *(Acer barbatum)* which looks like a smaller sugar maple. Two imported trees, the English field maple *(A. campestre)* and the hedge maple *(A. ginalla)*, are fine quick-result subjects. But the ones most often seen as bonsai are the Japanese maples. Greer Gardens (see list of sources, Chapter 20) lists almost a hundred varieties of Japanese maples, and there are many more. *A. japonica buergerianum*, the trident maple, is one of the most popular for it attains great age and adapts well to pot culture. The small leaves are three pointed and growth is twiggy. *A. japonicum atropurpureum* (Japanese red maple), *A. japonica* "Butterfly" and "Burgundy Lace," as well as *A. japonica aureum*, "Shishigashira" are all excellent varieties and offer a great variety of leaf colors, shapes, and sizes.

Winter protection

Most Japanese maples are hardy in zones 6–9.

Shaping

All maples make better specimens when leaf pruning is carried out at least once a year. The best time to do the job is when the first crop of leaves has developed and hardened off. (See Chapter 3, Leaf Pruning.) If wires are used watch carefully and remove them before they can mark the bark.

Location

Give full sun until midsummer, when they should be moved to a location with morning sun only or dappled sun.

Potting

The temptation to plant maples in very shallow pots is strong for they look especially fine in this type of pot, but if you do, use a mulch or ground cover for maples in shallow pots often show curled, seared leaves if the soil becomes too warm.

Maple seedlings may be collected in gardens and in the countryside. Start with seedlings about 12 to 18 inches (31–49 cm) high. Prune and pot, following the general instructions in Chapter 3.

MULBERRY *(Morus)*: **Zones vary. Any style except cascade.**

Not only are there many species of mulberry but they tend to cross, making identification very difficult. Most of the mulberries make smashing bonsai for the leaves dwarf well, growth is twiggy, results are quick, and they fruit willingly in pots. The berry, which looks a little like a blackberry, can be red, black, or white. Contrary to what we are often told, some fruits will dwarf and the mulberry is one of the obliging trees that gives us this valuable feature. The fruits and their stems dwarf beautifully, making one of the most attractive fruiting bonsai in a collection.

Wiring is not usually necessary. Young trees can be dug up at almost any time with a little ball of earth and potted for training. Since mulberries produce many seeds and birds carry them long distances, it's easy to find seedlings. Just look for a mature tree; there will be little ones nearby.

Mulberry leaves may be mitten shape or heart shape. Some are large, but these, too, will dwarf. We can't say whether one can or should leaf prune a mulberry. The leaves are often so small and the twigs so fine that we don't bother.

Red mulberry *(M. rubra)* is found throughout the eastern half of North America. It has a mitten-shaped or three-lobed leaf which is slightly crinkled and makes good surface roots which are brilliant orange when first uncovered, remaining so for a year or more. Texas mulberry *(M. microphylla)*, similar to red mulberry, is native to Texas and thereabouts. The leaf is much smaller and the fruit is round and black.

White *(M. alba)*, paper *(M. papyrifera)*, and black *(M. nigra)* mulberries are not native to this country but have been naturalized and are found throughout the eastern United States. All three adapt easily to bonsai culture, requiring no special care other than what need be given to any deciduous tree.

Location

They can take either full sun or morning sun but may show some leaf browning in midsummer; if so, move them to where they receive less light.

Some seed catalogues offer them as windbreak or hedging plants.

Winter protection

The Texas mulberry is probably the only type that needs more than standard winter protection; it should be wintered in a cold room.

Repotting

If they are not repotted faithfully each spring there may be some twig dieback the following winter.

Watering

Water when soil begins to look dry.

Soil

Use a 1–1–1 mix, as described in Chapter 12.

Feeding

Follow the program outlined in the chart, Chapter 10, for deciduous flowering trees.

Shaping

Very little wiring is needed. Fruiting takes place all along the branches so they can be nipped to retain shape throughout the growing season.

MULTIFLORA ROSE: Zones 3–8, all styles especially cascade, informal upright, root-over-rock, stilt-root, or cloud.

Used as a root stock for nursery roses since the early 1800s, deservedly lauded as "The Living Stock Fence—Hog-Tight" (true) in the 1940s, praised by conservationists for game cover and erosion control and forever after cursed and combated as a pesky weed, the multiflora rose makes a fascinating bonsai. Being a rose, it does have compound leaves but they dwarf well and the flowers and fruit are in good scale.

The small, five-petaled white or pinkish flowers are delicate and bloom over a long period. The foliage is resistant to disease. The trunk of a young plant can be increased nicely in a few years or you can start with quite a large plant and prune and wire it into a unique specimen (see figs. 6–1, 2).

Location

When growth is well established give full sun.

Watering

Water as you would any other deciduous. Never let a rose dry out.

Soil

Use one part loam, one part clay soil, one part sand.

Feeding

Feed 5–10–7 at ½ strength every two weeks except for winter and midsummer, when roses must rest. This program will help to shorten leaf nodes and make for more compact, slower growth. If growth is too coarse, on the recommended two-week schedule, feed less often.

Shaping

Prune after flowering, leaving a few old flower heads to mature into hips, which are small, round, red—and very pretty. Do not allow all flowers to produce seeds or you will lose the opportunity to shape the plant before the next year's bloom. Discontinue all feeding and pruning six to eight weeks before hard frosts are expected.

Since multiflora is a rampant grower, tending toward arching briar vines, frequent pinching of buds is necessary through the spring, but give a few branches opportunity to grow and set buds.

Buds will break all over the trunk, giving plenty to choose from. Put any drastic pruning to the back, of course. Always paint all cuts with white glue or acrylic paint. This protects them from bees, who often bore several inches into unprotected pith to lay their eggs, killing the stem as far as the burrow extends.

Problems

Multifloras are disease resistant but if an occasional attack of mildew or black-spot appears, use Benlate (trade name for Benomyl). Extended wet weather aggravates this problem so it may be necessary to treat the plant after every rain. Aphids love roses; control them with detergent solution or Malathion (see Insecticides, Chapter 16).

They do have thorns, but what is a rose without a thorn?

NATAL PLUM (*Carissa grandiflora*): **Zones 8–10. Cascade, semi-cascade, many other styles.**

The natal plum is often advertised with "bonsai" stuck somewhere in its name—not correct but not a bad idea, since the tree is such a likely subject for the art (fig. 11–20).

The bark is furrowed and grayish even in fairly young specimens. The trunk and branches are irregular, curving into graceful shapes. The leaves are small, round, and waxy (especially on *C. grandiflora* "Boxwood") and are in clusters. The natal plum blooms over much of the season with fragrant white stars and bears large, edible, purple-red plums which stay on the plant a long time. When seeded, sliced, and cooked into a syrup with sugar and lemon juice they make a great ice-cream topping.

Location

A nice houseplant if you can provide enough sun. Outdoors grow it in full sun or at least morning sun.

Feeding

Give any broadleaf evergreen food at ½ strength monthly from the beginning of the growing season until midsummer. Give 0–7–10 at ½ strength or something similar once or twice in the fall at four week intervals.

General care

Follow the same instructions as for jasmine.

11–20 *Carissa* natal plum 12 inches high.

PINE *(Pinus):* **Zones vary with species. Most styles are appropriate.**

Many people think of pine when they think of bonsai, for these trees make the loveliest, most impressive specimens one can imagine. Pine needles grow in bundles of from two to five needles except for the single-leaf pine (*Pinus monophylla*) which is not generally used in bonsai.

There are over thirty species of pines native to North America ranging through all zones. Some are wonderfully suited to our use, although many are not because of their very long needles or other features.

Repotting

All young pines are more vulnerable to disease and damage from weather and transplanting than older trees and should be handled with care. Drastic root pruning may kill them so at repotting time take about one quarter the root mass only and balance the root loss with comparable top pruning.

Soil

Use the standard soil mix, with the addition of an extra part of sand. In potting, pat down the soil firmly but gently, making sure all roots are in snug contact with soil.

Feeding

Consult the Seasonal Fertilizing Chart in Chapter 10.

BRISTLECONE PINE

From our western mountains, *Pinus aristata* is known to attain great age, with some living specimens estimated to be 4,000 years old! The needles are short, in bundles of five, dotted with bits of dried white resin. It's an excellent bonsai candidate. It thrives in zones 4–6. As with all pines, do not overwater. (Fig. 11–21.)

PINYON PINE

The *P. edulis* and *cembroides* are also good short-needled candidates. The pinyon pine is sensitive to cold and is best suited to zones 7–9.

MONTEREY PINE

A tree with short needles in bundles of two or three, a dense black crown, fissured bark, and a natural tendency to develop a windswept style, the *P. radiata*, also makes a fine bonsai. It is native to zone 10.

SCOTCH PINE

Introduced from Europe, the Scotch pine (*P. sylvestris*) is one of the most cooperative of the pine family. It is easy to transplant, and, if gradually pruned back, it is one of the few pines that can initiate new buds of old wood. It thrives in zones 4–7. (Fig. 11–22.)

Shaping

In early spring, the short buds formed the previous year lengthen into candles on which needles begin to develop. As soon as you can begin to see individual needles, but before they loosen from the candle, break them off, leaving no more than three or four. (If a longer branch is desired, leave more needles.) This candle is the entire growth for the season. If it is not pruned the tree is soon a rambling, undisciplined specimen, without the close, bunchy branches that give a pine so much bonsai appeal. Do not cut the needles to make them shorter as this makes the tree ugly. (The long needles of the Japanese black pine are accepted and are not considered inappropriate.)

Most pine branches will finally die if cut back beyond visible buds for very few can initiate new buds on old, mature wood. Branches of most pines are slow to take the position given them with wiring and usually grow so much that the wires must be removed and replaced several times. It's not unusual to see old pines with training wires.

Heavy pruning during or just before the growing season causes an excessive loss of sap so prune large branches in late fall or during the winter. Allow the wound to dry for a few days then paint with acrylic paint (you can match the bark color) or Elmer's glue.

Feeding

Consult the Seasonal Fertilizing Chart on pines and spruces, Chapter 10.

Watering

Soak the roots well when the entire soil surface looks dry. Do not keep the soil wet.

Location

Pines will grow in full sun or morning sun and afternoon shade.

POMEGRANATE, DWARF POMEGRANATE *(Punica granatum, Punica granatum nana)*: **Zones 7–8, also 9, but does not fruit well at 9. Grove, formal and informal upright, root-connected grove.**

Marble-size fruit in good scale, brilliant red-orange flowers, tiny narrow leaves, striated bark, quick development, good surface roots in a few years—all this and more are found in the dwarf pomegranate (fig. 11–23). The standard pomegranate is also fine for bonsai but with the one drawback of large fruit.

Shaping

Use paper-wrapped wires for what little wiring may be necessary, leaving them on less than six weeks. Most training 1s accomplished with pruning and weights. Since pomegranates bloom at the ends of new shoots, only prune immediately after flowering.

Soil

We suggest two parts fine sharp sand, one part sphagnum, and one part loam. Drainage must be good.

11-21 Bristle cone pine, 11 inches. *(Joel Gold collection. Cleo Stephens, photo)*

11-22 An old Scotch pine "Lochmoor," 27 inches. *(Dunton collection)*

119

Feeding

Provide ¼ strength Rapid-Gro every two weeks as soon as new growth begins in spring, discontinue during midsummer heat, then in early fall give two feedings of 0–7–5 at ½ strength three weeks apart.

Location

Pomegranates can thrive in full sun, but must not dry out. In zones 8–10 they can be left outdoors year round and can be repotted at the beginning of the growing season. In all other zones they should be stored in a cold (above freezing) room where they will go dormant. Repot when buds begin to swell as spring approaches. They can make pretty houseplants in winter, but are vulnerable to mites, mealy bugs, and aphids, and must have strong light.

Propagation

The plant is easy to propagate by cuttings or seed; the seed remains viable for three years.

QUINCE *(Chaenomeles):* **Zones 4–8. Any style.**

Quinces flower early in the spring in many shades of red through pink to white (fig. 11–24), with occasionally a repeat bloom in late summer. Flowers are paler when allowed to open out of the sun.

Old quinces from a nursery or the lawn can be successfully cut down to pot-size if top and roots are both pruned to balance. It will take several years to develop fine twigs from an old plant, but since even old branches initiate flower buds, you'll have flowers to enjoy from the first spring.

Repotting

The proper time is in the fall as soon as leaves drop.

Feeding

Fertilize as for deciduous fruit trees. Quince is a heavy feeder and will go completely bare and dormant in late summer if feeding and conscientious watering is neglected. Unless the tree is very large and vigorous do not allow more than two or three fruits to develop and pick them off early. They take a great amount of nourishment that could better be stored for next year's blooms.

Location

In spring, a full day of sun is beneficial, but when summer heat becomes intense, move to a dappled sun or only morning sun.

Winter protection

Protect as for any deciduous in its zone range. The plants are very hardy and

11-23 Pomegranate, 5 inches.

11-24 Detail of growth characteristic of Chinese quince.

reliable, and are such excellent bonsai subjects that everyone could enjoy several colors and species.

Soil

Use 1 part builder's sand, 1 part loam, one part black peat. When collecting the plant it's best to take along plenty of the native muck in which it is growing.

Location

Full sun or partial shade.

Watering

Water when soil begins to look dry. Uses a lot of water.

Feeding

Fertilize in spring and midsummer with ½ strength Hyponex.

RED MANGROVE *(Rhizophora mangie):* **Zones 9–10. Has its own distinctive style.**

Called the walking, island-building tree and protected by law, the red mangrove is a very curious-looking specimen. Standing on spreading stilt-roots, it is forever sending down roots from its trunk or branches. Each root develops its own trunk and branches which send down yet another root until whole jungles are formed. These trees always grow at the edge of salt water and the hanging roots are often encrusted with barnacles and oysters. We know that they can grow for several years without salt water, but we have been mixing aquarium-supply synthetic salts for ours, which lost most of their leaves when transplanted then releafed with smaller ones.

The leaves are a long oval, 3 to 5 inches (7.8–13 cm) in length with a rubbery, shiny appearance.

The seeds germinate while still on the tree. Long cigar-like green shoots emerge from the seeds which then drop off, plummet into the soft mud, and take root or float until they can find a suitable rooting medium.

The flowers are small and yellow and the bark is gray to gray-brown, furrowed, and scaly. The basic tree form in nature is broad and low, spreading to a maximum of about twenty feet (6 meters).

Propagation

Mangrove trees can be started from the prolific seeds (see fig. 2–15) or dug from the wild. In young trees such as these shown (fig. 11–25) there is little root development under the sand, and they are transplanted easily.

11-25 Red mangrove, 20 inches, growing at canal edge in Florida. Note oysters and barnacles on roots.

SERISSA *(Serissa foetida flora plena):* **Zones 9-10. Any style.**

This is another plant that seems just made for training as a bonsai of tiny (*mamé* and smaller) or medium sizes. It isn't a large plant, possibly reaching only 24 inches (61 cm) in Florida and California, where it is often used as a low, broad landscaping shrub.

When it's happy, bloom is almost constant. It bears tiny, white, single or double flowers. The leaves are also tiny, measuring about ¼ inch (less than 1 cm), and can be deep green or green and white variegated.

Location

Give morning sun and afternoon shade, or dappled sun.

Feeding

Follow the same schedule as for Carissa (Natal Plum).

Watering

Keep moist, but not soggy.

Shaping

The process of wiring and pruning can continue throughout the year.

SPRUCE *(Picea sp.):* **Most hardy zones 2 or 3 through 6. Good for formal and informal upright styles.**

The many varieties of spruce are interesting bonsai candidates because most of them have such very short needles, are not difficult to train, and respond quickly to pruning. Landscape nurseries, probably the best place to get them, abound with *Picea* species. (figs. 11–26, 27, 28.)

Watering

Spruce are more tolerant of overwatering than pines, but should be given the same care.

Shaping

The new buds form a round soft tassel of needles which, as they develop, gradually push off their brown covering. Before or immediately after it is dropped, reach into the center of the tassel and twist out most of the needles. Take care that the entire tassel is not broken off. Never cut new needles. Most spruces have dormant buds all along their stems, but it's risky to completely remove the new bud (see figs. 3–4, 5). Wire and train as for pines.

Soil

Use the standard mix.

Location

Put in full sun.

TEXAS EBONY *(Pithecollobium flexicaule):* **Zones 8–9. Any style except root-over-rock or cascade.**

The naturally zigzagging branches and featherlike leaves made this tree a pretty bonsai. It is easy to maintain, develops quickly in its adolescent phase, and is a good plant for the house.

Feeding
Feed 12–12–12, ½ strength in spring as buds loosen and every three weeks thereafter until midsummer heat; stop until temperature moderates then give one more feeding full strength.

Location
The plant may be kept outdoors until temperature sinks to 45° F. (8° C.) at night; then place it in a sunny window or under gro-lites.

Repotting
This should be done in late spring as new buds loosen.

Watering
Keep moist.

Soil
Use two parts sand, one part garden loam, one part black peat.

Shaping
Keep pruning throughout the growing season.

WILLOW *(Salix sp.):* **Zones 3–9, depending upon species. Cascade style for weeping willows, almost any style for others.**
The arctic and alpine willows make interesting small-leaved companions for saikei plants but seldom develop the heavy trunks we desire for bonsai.

Weeping willows, however, can be sensational specimens, standing on tall pedestals with weeping branches as much as six feet in length. Our native willows also are good possibilities, for they develop quickly, with a bark that is nicely patterned on younger trees.

Pruning
Any attempt to shorten the branches results in erratic brushes at the pruned point so leave the branches long and thin them out at the trunk for a graceful shape. The willow grows rapidly and if not pruned almost daily is soon out of control. Reducing leaf and branch volume restricts growth.

Watering
Keep the pot base in about two inches of water during the growing season.

11-26 Colorado blue spruce, 22 inches. (*Ann Pipe collection. Cleo Stephens, photo*)

11-27 Colorado blue spruce,
15 inches. *(Ann Pipe collection.*
Cleo Stephens, photo)

11-28 Spruce, 12 inches. *(Ann Pipe collection. Cleo Stephens, photo)*

Repotting

Repot both spring and fall, for root growth is rampant. Otherwise, culture is as for any deciduous.

Location

Give morning sun only or dappled sun all day.

Feeding

Fertilize as for standard deciduous. Consult Seasonal Fertilizing Chart, Chapter 10.

WISTERIA *(Wisteria sp.):* **Zones 5–9. Best as cascade or informal weeping upright style.**

The beautiful wisteria is an easy and rewarding subject for bonsai, displaying long, graceful drooping cymes of flowers in spring and clear yellow foliage in fall.

Watering

Culture is exactly as for quince but in midsummer the pot should be set in a shallow tray of water and kept moist at all times.

Shaping

Wisteria grows so rampantly that the vines must be constantly cut back, leaving only one or two sets of the compound leaves. Blooms appear on old wood, sometimes even far back on a large thick branch, so pruning can be done with no fear of losing flowers.

Repotting

This should be done in spring and again in fall as root growth is especially vigorous.

Location

Wisteria enjoys full sun except in the hottest part of the summer when it may show scorched leaf edges and tips. This is the time to move it to dappled sun to make sure it does not suffer for lack of water.

Feeding

Provide 5–10–10 at ½ strength monthly, beginning as the buds loosen. Stop in midsummer, then give 5–10–10 ½ strength as weather begins to cool, and 0–7–10 ½ strength three weeks later.

12. Planting Your Bonsai

SOILS

There is a raging controversy about the most suitable soils and how to process them for bonsai; the reason is that there is a wide variation in what most plants will tolerate and that many growers confuse bare survival with successful horticulture.

When a plant is taken from the wild, plenty of extra soil from the original site can be obtained for repotting. Another strategy is to study the color and texture of the native soil so a formula can be made up that duplicates it in looks and performance. This also can be done with nursery plants but sooner or later the time will come when the grower wants to find out for himself just what soils are most suitable for each of the plants in his collection. Most greenhouses will sell potting soil or it can be bought at any garden supply store but it is much more satisfactory to make your own.

STANDARD SOIL MIX

Most soil mixtures are given in "parts"—an easy-to-understand method which is clear enough and precise enough for anyone to follow. There is a classic formula which we call our standard mix for use when there is any doubt:

• One part sand: sharp builder's sand, *not* from the seashore.
• One part loam: any darkish garden soil high enough in organic matter to support healthy vegetables, grass, flowers, or weeds.
• One part peat: here there is a little variation. Both Michigan peat, which is black,

fine, and partially decomposed, and brown sphagnum peat, which is a little coarser, can be used. Except for azaleas, we always use the brown. Long-fiber sphagnum peat is too coarse for potting mixtures.

Compost is often used instead of peat, but it is an unknown quantity at best and some weed killer could be carried through in grass clippings or weed leaves. If you decide to use compost be well acquainted with its source and do remember it's not acid enough for some plants, such as azaleas.

The "parts" can be measured with a tin can, bushel basket, whatever—so long as each part is equal. The word "part" means the same as "measure" or "portion."

SIFTING

To sift or not to sift is a question much discussed in bonsai circles—the answer is maybe. Sifted soil often does produce better, more predictable results but with some plants the effect is negligible. Yes, it is better to sift but there is no need to delay a needed potting when there isn't time to sift and mix in the usual way. As a general practice we sift soil for all our trees but if we should have to repot a single plant (not during the usual wholesale repotting time) we may mix up something quickly and make do.

Sifting is suggested to make sure the soil drains properly. Sets of soil sifters are sold in garden supply stores, hardware store garden departments, and bonsai supply houses. You easily can make a set, using wooden frames with screening of various sizes: ¼-, ⅛-, and 1⁄16-inch holes. Tack or staple the screen sandwiched between two frames to make it more secure. The screening will soon pull away from the frame without some sort of reinforcement. Make the sifters large enough—at least 18 inches (46 cm) wide and long. One clever handyman contrived his large and medium screen frames to fit exactly over the plastic trash cans he used to hold the soil-mix components. Since the dust that passes through the last screening is discarded, you don't need a separate can for this size.

To sift:

1. Use the large-size screen first, discarding all clods and debris too large to pass through.

2. Then use the middle-size, keeping the soil that does not pass through to put into the pot first as the bottom layer of soil.

3. Sift the soil which went through the middle screen, saving the soil which does not pass through for the main potting soil. Either discard the dust that passes through or save a little of it for a light dusting over the surface of soil used as a rooting medium for powdered moss.

Sift the loam and peat separately and then mix—do not sift after blending the components. You probably won't have to sift the sand as there is no need to remove the finest grains.

Sifting and blending potting soil are chores you can accomplish when other work is slack. Store the blended soil mix or the separate components in plastic trash cans with lids. You may want to have four containers—one for each component to custom mix, and one with ready-to-go standard mix.

For the soil preferences of individual species, see Chapter 11, Favorite Trees for Bonsai.

STERILIZING SOIL

This is a good idea when there is danger that insects or disease are carried in the soil. Sterilization can be done in an oven heated to 250° F. (120° C.) for thirty minutes or with a good soaking in one of the soil-insect poisons. Experiments are being conducted with No Pest Strips laid on the surface of the soil in a tightly closed container. However, results are not proven and there might be some danger from the fumes. Use caution if you try it. Some greenhouses use a fumigant, which is too dangerous for the average grower to handle, and some use steam.

COMPOST

Composting organic matter is an ancient practice which has recently come back into popularity—a status not completely deserved. If one is willing to go to all the necessary bother, a product results which may be slightly superior to Michigan peat.

Since its nutrient content and pH analyses are unknown, it's wise to test compost. It's common to overestimate the nutrient value; actually it is comparable to Michigan or sphagnum moss as a soil conditioner. However, there is some satisfaction to be gained from creating a nice black growing medium from debris and scraps!

Any organic matter can be used—kitchen scraps, grass clippings, leaves, shredded newspapers, and animal manures. You can even use diseased plant remains, because if the proper heating from fermentation takes place, all dangerous spores, insect eggs, and weed seeds will be destroyed. Never use grass or weeds that may have been treated with weed killer or you may be in for an unpleasant surprise.

The compost bins sold by garden supply companies are neat, useful investments. Buy the sturdiest one for some are tinny and flimsy and rust out in the first year. One problem is that most prefab compost bins are too small—a manageable size would be around 4 × 4 feet (1.2 m).

The function of the bin is to furnish vertical walls which keep the pile from becoming a rounded heap that sheds rain. The compost mass should be lower at the middle to keep the material damp, thus encouraging fermentation. Locate your compost heap in a shady place. There will be some odor for a time, much like that of a neglected stable, so don't place it where your neighbor will complain.

Begin to build the heap in spring. Each 6–10 inch (16–21 cm) layer should be well packed down and, if dry, watered. Toss on a mixture of sulphate of ammonia and superphosphate of lime, using about ½ ounce (a little less than 2 grams) for each square yard (.8361 sq. meters) of compost. Or use a proprietary decay accelerator (available at nurseries under various brand names). Add animal manure, sawdust, wood ashes, and whatever else is handy and follow with about an inch (2.6 cm) of soil. Continue to add layer upon layer of compost and additives to a height of 3 or 4 feet (.9–1.2 meters) and finish with about 4–6 inches (10–15 cm) of soil. Do not add hard woody chunks unless they've been burned to ashes.

After five to seven weeks turn the pile. Start by digging a trench along one side, throwing the compost over to the opposite side of the pit. Dig a second trench beside the first, throwing the contents of the second trench upside down into the first trench. Continue across the area, methodically emptying the contents from each new trench upside down as filling into the empty trench beside it. Level the mass, leaving the middle lower to retain rainfall. Dampen if necessary and cover with 2–3 inches of soil. It's ready for use at this point, but ideally it should be left to "work" for another two weeks.

This process produces a fine soil conditioner to be used as the humus component of soil mixtures or as a good mulch. It's best to sift the material through a coarse sieve before blending it with other components.

Or you can buy a nice, sterile cubic-yard bale of milled brown sphagnum moss. It's a lot less work!

REPOTTING

HOW TO REPOT

The picture series below (figs. 12-1—19) shows the steps to be taken in repotting. We used a Catlin elm as an example but the general procedure would be the same for all trees.

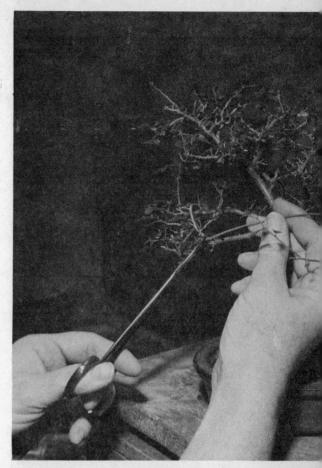

12–1 Catlin elm is a good subject but tends to grow long horizontal branches. This one is 6 inches high.

12–2, 3, 4 Begin by pruning top to shape. Remove moss.

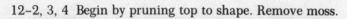

12-5 Place fingers over soil, turn upside down, tap edge of pot against a wooden edge if necessary to loosen soil.

12-6 Push out if necessary.

12-7 The overgrown root mass. Set aside in a protected area away from sun and wind.

12-8, 9, 10 Prepare pot; place screen, sand, and soil in bottom.

12-11, 12 Untangle roots.

12-13 Reduce root mass, always using *sharp* scissors or pruners.

12-17 Clean up, then set pot in room-temperature water just to the rim until top of soil is moist. We like to use root stimulater in the water, mixed as directed or a little weaker. Keep plant moist and out of sun and wind until new growth starts, then gradually give more sun.

12-14 Place in prepared pot. Work soil around roots with pencil or chopstick. Firm gently. Some growers like to tie the tree down at this point by running wires up through drainage holes and over the roots, but we seldom find it necessary. A few soft cloth strips can be passed under the pot and around the branches if wind is a problem, or if the tree is not balanced enough to stay firm. The strips should be removed in two or three weeks.

12-18 Three months later.

12–15 Firm and shape soil gently.

12–16 Replace moss.

12–19 When a plant has a very dense root mass (azaleas are an example), take out pie-shaped segments as shown. Top sketch; remove three or four segments this year, other segments next year (dotted wedge). Comb out and reduce roots and prune top as shown in lower drawing.

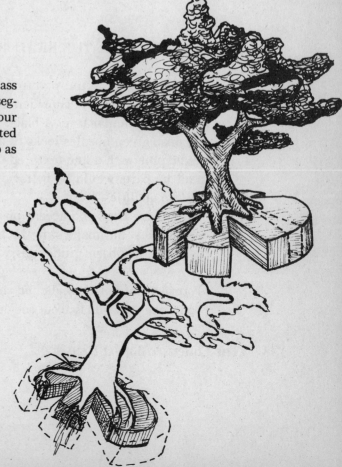

13. Choosing Pots and Tools

CONTAINERS

The bonsai pots imported from China and Japan are of a hard, fine-textured, fired clay. Although the prices charged for them have risen recently they are still a fine buy (see sources list, Chapter 20). Unlike ordinary domestic pots they seldom crack or flake even under the worst freezing and thawing conditions of winter. There are some exceptions though: The glazed pots with thinner walls will often crack in a freezing and thawing situation, and some of the round, porous, red clay Japanese training pots absorb moisture and break or flake off badly. Any pot which breaks will expose root ends to weather and drying which may cause the death of all or part of a tree.

CHOOSING JUST THE RIGHT POT

As a frame is to the painting, so is a pot to the bonsai. In selecting a pot proportion is the first consideration: choose the proper size and visual weight for each particular tree. A black pine with a heavy, dark, well-textured trunk and deep green needles looks best in a thick-walled, heavy-appearing pot. A 5-needle pine with a fine-textured trunk, small, short needles, and of small scale in all its parts would be better displayed in a pot of lighter weight and more delicate qualities.

Flowering trees and accent plants usually are best complemented by glazed, colored pots. But make sure the plant is not outshone by the color or design of the pot. A few basic guidelines:

• Formal or informal upright and single, two-trunk or triple-trunk styles usually look best if the pot width is about one-third the height of the tree with branches extending not too far over one or both edges; the overall depth of the pot should be about one and one-half times the width of the trunk; the pot color should always be subservient to color and texture of the tree—neutral shades are a good choice.

• Slanting or sinuous tree styles can be matched with pots by the same rules as above.
• Cascade style pots should emphasize the shape of this tree; the depth of the pot may be about one-half to three-fourths the height of the tree. Its width should be one-half to two-thirds the width of the branch spread. The matching of tree and pot must be sight-balanced because of the wide variation in design of the cascade style.
• Groves are best displayed in very shallow, rectangular or oval pots of a width about one and one-half times the height of the tallest tree.

When selecting a pot for a specific tree, it may help to use cardboard mock-ups. Study the dimensions of the most likely pots then construct simple models of them. Let's say the pot you favor is 16 inches (41 cm) long, 10 inches (21 cm) wide, and 2½ inches (6 cm) high. (If you're ordering from a catalogue, remember that the dimensions are given for inside the pot.) Make a cardboard rectangle of 16¼ by 10¼ inches and fold along the 16-inch side, allowing, say, 2½ inches outside dimensions for the height. If the pot is shown with feet, allow for this as well (fig. 13–1). Cut the cardboard to include any curve or slant shown on the sides. Try it on your tree—stand back and view it from a distance.

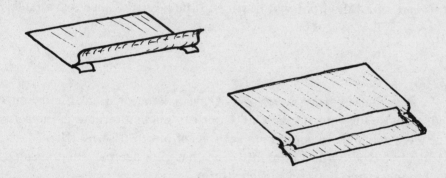

13–1 Top two drawings—a quick mock-up of a rectangular pot. Do it in scale so that you'll know what to expect when the pot you order arrives. Bottom two drawings—paper-clip this mock-up together to get a realistic idea of how an oval pot would look. Try it on the tree.

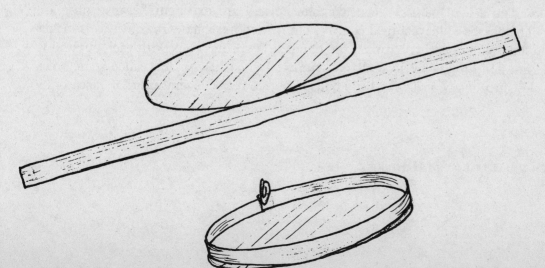

139

For an oval or round pot, follow the same methods, but cut the width piece long enough to go completely around the circumference of the pot, and fasten with a paper clip.

Color is important. It's wise to color your mock-up with tempera, pastels, watercolors, or even crayons to duplicate the design and color of the pot. A bonsai tree looks very different in, say, deep brown-red as compared to white or glazed blue.

A pot should not make the tree look cramped and uncomfortable, nor should a tree look lost and overwhelmed by a too-large pot. Of course, size is not quite as important for a tree whose trunk is still to be enlarged before potting in its final exhibition pot. We're talking here of a finished bonsai whose shape and size are ready for viewing. This is not to say any bonsai is ever "finished." It actually is in training and development its entire life no matter how ancient it becomes—but aren't we all?

TOOLS AND EQUIPMENT

Most of the tools sold for bonsai use are pruners of one kind or another. There is a pruning tool tailored for every need, from *mamé* twigs to heavy branches and roots (fig. 13–2). (See Sources list, Chapter 20, for bonsai tools.) As we discuss the use of each tool we'll make suggestions for possible substitution; few of us can afford the luxury of buying all the beautiful pieces available.

SCISSORS

First, you will need straight scissors—they make a good clean cut and are fairly all-purpose for your needs. Our American-made alternate is the scissor-blade pruners available in equipment sections of most nurseries. Don't buy the blade-and-anvil type, with a straight blade that cuts against a flat surface; it crushes branches, and leaves a ragged stump.

BITE CUTTERS

The several sizes of concave bite cutters are excellent because they are engineered to leave a neat concave cut, which heals flat. One of these is rather small with a spring between the handles. It springs back with each cut and is fine for nipping little buds off trunks—a good, useful tool since some trees produce many dozens of little buds on a tree trunk several times in a season.

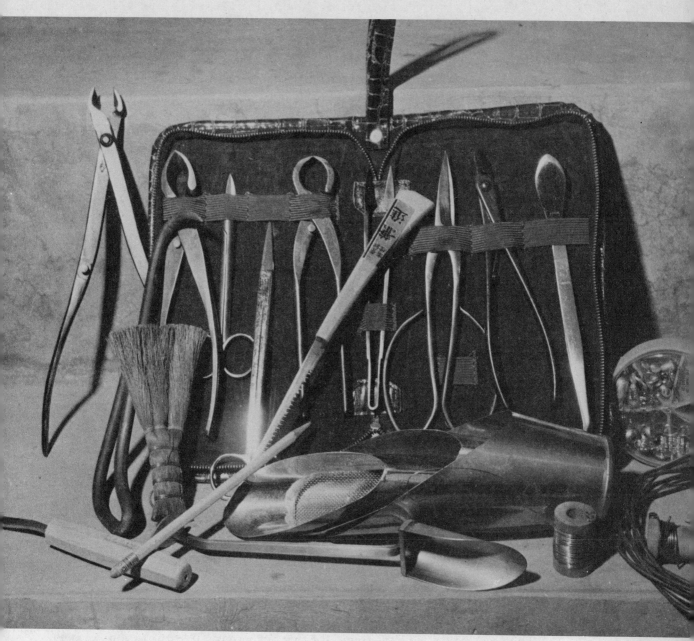

13-2 Tools make the work easier. Left to right, *top row:* long-handled concave-bite cutters, small jaws, larger bite cutters, pine gather-bud shears, stainless steel surgeon's scissors for all-round pruning, root-knot cutter, leaf pruner, large scissors, spring-back bud nippers for buds on trunk and branches, tweezer-spatula, lead weights. *Bottom row:* carving tool, root hook, palm fiber whisk, pencil for working soil into root crevasses, small branch saw, scoops (nested ones have built-in sifters), various sizes of copper wire, lead weights.

ROOT-KNOT CUTTERS

Root-knot cutters are very strong; they are made to remove disfiguring overgrown knots, big branches, and heavy roots. On a large root or knot, they can make several bites, side by side. Never twist the jaws of the cutter to release it from the wood; hold the handle of the jaw that is stuck and rock it loose gently. Bolt cutters from the hardware store are not half as good, but if the blades are ground down on the concave side and are well-sharpened they are the nearest approximation.

LEAF CUTTERS

These enable one to cut hundreds of leaf stems with a minimum of blisters and tiredness, because they are light-weight, precise, and spring open with just the right resilience after each cut. Barber shears aren't too bad a substitute but after leaf cutting one medium tree you'll have blisters and tired, cramped hands. There is a similar tool, offered by fishermen's supply companies, for clipping monofilament line. Good sporting goods stores usually have them and they're listed as "nippers."

SMALL PRUNERS

Mamé pruners are for the tiniest trees and are fun to have but cuticle scissors are almost as good.

SHEARS

Pine gather-bud shears are for cutting pine candles as they elongate. They are fashioned with long handles and fairly short jaws. Of course, any scissors will do this job or you can snap the candles with your fingers.

The best scissors we have found for this purpose is a beautiful stainless-steel piece. The jaws are furnished with shallow non-slip teeth. It was the discovery of a fellow bonsai grower who is a surgeon. This tool isn't as cheap as its bonsai-tool counterpart but, being stainless steel, it can be left on the bench for those daily nipping chores with no worry about its rusting.

TWEEZERS

Several different shapes of tweezers are available, my favorite being a large stainless-steel model with angled jaws and a spatula at the back end. This is extremely useful in grooming; it cleans out leaves, brown needles, and debris from the ground cover; it breaks off the end of spruce buds without breaking or bruising the remaining needles; it apprehends insects; and it is excellent for reaching down on the sides of weed crowns and pulling them out without breaking off their roots. Tweezers have more uses than we can list. Even the spatula end is useful to remove and replace moss and to tamp and shape the soil surface.

Hardware stores, surgeon's supply companies, and mechanic's shops have long, strong tweezers but we know of none that have the spatula end which you can get at a bonsai supply house.

SAWS

Pruning saws are for dealing with the branch or root that just won't yield to cutting tools. Bonsai tool companies have different sizes of saws, some straight, some with blades that fold into the handles. The edge opposite the teeth is sharpened—not for cutting, but so that the blade will go easily through the wood without binding. The pruning saw cuts as you pull and is not like our carpenter's saws which cut as they are pushed. You may need several sizes. Even with careful from-small-seedling training, a large branch may die and need to be removed or a taproot may knot, swell, and distort. Our American-made pruning saws are fine for orchards but leave a rough, bark-damaged edge. Sometimes you can start and finish a cut with a small saw but do the middle, largest part of the cut with a larger saw.

GOUGES, KNIVES

Gouges must be used to give a sunken, concave shape after a saw is used. It's very important to hollow any saw cut since it will not heal flat otherwise (see fig. 4–5).

Buy a sharpening stone when you buy the gouge and keep it well sharpened; dull blades slip, requiring more force, and the job won't be as smooth. It's useful to have a set of bonsai gouging and carving tools. They can be from bonsai supply stores or from hobby supply houses individually or in sets. They can be very effective pieces or cheap, flimsy shams. The blade should be sturdy, tapering sharply to a keen edge, not tinny and thin with a blade that will flex.

The carving job can be done with a knife or the rounded, sharp end of a kitchen potato peeler, but not as well or as easily as with good bonsai tools.

If you do any carving do not jab the wood—use a steady pressure, and rock the blade from side to side, cutting grooves until the cut area is a smooth, shallow depression. If the wound is a big one (an inch or more), leave a point of fiber at the center. The pruning wound should be an oval shape, pointed at each end and running lengthwise, not round, across the trunk or branch.

The edges of the bark should be smoothed and shaped. Sometimes tapering must be done to blend trunk into branch. For this a florist's knife is good. It has a rigid blade with a straight, sharp edge. Joel Gould uses a veterinarian's knife (see figs. 4–5, 6).

A knife is also necessary if you suspect borers. Caught in time, they can be dug out.

PLIERS

Jin pliers are designed to grasp branches and bark, to break the branch and to peel away the bark. Hardware store pliers (or the ones in the kitchen utility tool drawer) will do the job, or course, but the jin pliers are easier to use; their jaws are shaped perfectly for the purpose.

Needle-nosed pliers, from very small jeweler's pliers to the largest mechanic's grippers, simplify and expedite wiring and unwiring chores. They can reach between branches where fingers cannot and are virtually indispensable. Find them in hardware, hobby, craft, and bonsai supply companies.

WEIGHTS

Lead weights (fishing supply store, again), can be used for training branches where wiring is impractical. Select the desired size from the handy sectioned dispenser, attach it to an S hanger made of copper wire and hook it on—then there's no worry about removing wire! Shift the position of the S hanger frequently and check to see that the weight doesn't cause a branch to whip about in a high wind.

WIRE

Many sizes of copper wire will be needed (see Chapter 3, Wiring). Wire can be found in hardware shops or bonsai supply stores. You can also ask for leftover scraps from building sites. Do not use iron wire which will rust and injure branches, or aluminum wire, which conducts heat and cold and is either too soft or too brittle, depending upon type. Among its virtues, copper is the most unobtrusive in color once it oxidizes slightly.

WIRE CUTTERS

Several sizes of strong, short-jawed wire cutters, which may be found in hardware stores or bonsai supply catalogues, are necessary. After being heat-softened (annealed) and used, copper wire hardens and is difficult to remove in one piece without injuring the tree. Instead, cut it off by nipping each turn of wire and remove the pieces that don't drop off with tweezers or needle-nosed pliers. Do not scratch the bark during wire removal. We believe the common, garden-variety cutters are entirely adequate, and in view of this, the ones from bonsai supply companies seem unrealistically expensive. Their only real advantage is they are shaped in such a way that they are less likely to cut bark accidentally.

ROOT COMBERS

Several kinds of root-combing devices are shown in bonsai tool catalogues to disentangle roots so that they may be cut and arranged. One might chop away the edges of a block of roots and set the undisturbed mass back in a pot, but this would soon produce a mat of congested dead roots that water, air, and nutrients could not penetrate.

Some of the combing devices are three-pronged. However, our preferred tool is a simple, sharpened iron hook (see figs. 5–11, 12–11, 12) similar to a dock-worker's cargo hook. It is strong, yet soil can be removed and roots pulled out of the round-and-round pattern they have established with a minimum of bruising and tearing. A stout, sharpened stick or, for smaller trees, a sharpened chopstick or pencil would serve as possible alternatives. A pencil can be used but it should have a short, rounded lead or it will break off and make a jagged root-damaging weapon.

TOOL KITS

To hold all these tools and keep them neatly organized, fitted kits are available. They look very much like a woman's flat, book-style purse. They have a loop handle, and can be zipped closed. We can contrive no close approximation of this convenient device but alternatives are endless.

For a dollar or two there are plastic tool carriers—shallow open-top boxes divided into compartments with a carrying handle in the middle. You will find them at variety and hardware stores and kitchen-supply departments. They are made for holding household cleaning equipment and small gardening tools.

Plastic fishing-tackle boxes also are useful, especially the ones that open out to display numerous trays, all at one's fingertips. Buy one with many more compartments than you have tools—you'll need them for all the indispensables you will accumulate as time goes by.

Carpenter's aprons put everything at hand. You can make your own of canvas or any heavy cloth, leather, or Ultrasuede (a brand name for an expensive fabric which looks like the finest suede and is very sturdy and washable).

CARE OF TOOLS

Any tool worth buying must be kept clean, sharpened, and rust free (most tools made for bonsai rust easily). Clean with alcohol or nail-polish remover after each use and oil with Three-in-One or something similar.

Other reasons for faithful cleaning are: that the juices of some plants are unfriendly to others, that diseases and pests can be spread by dirty tools, and that a dull, resin-clogged tool won't perform well.

To sharpen pruners use a fine-grained honing stone moistened with water or light oil. Hone only the free side of the blade, never the surfaces that touch, because if blades don't bypass one another closely, they won't cut. Do not hone from the outside to the sharp inside of the blade. This will cause a hairline of metal to turn to the other side of the cutting edge, defeating your purpose for then you would have to grind from the wrong side of the blade to remove the turned metal. Think of it this way: You are pushing the metal away from the edge to sharpen it. Hone in one direction only—don't file back and forth.

A properly maintained tool seldom wears out. Buy the best you can afford, keep them clean and oiled, and you'll enjoy using them for many years.

We have described the uses, sources, and care of only a few of the available tools. Branch splitters, jacks, branch benders, and so on aren't mentioned because they are not in general use. As the grower gets more deeply into the art of bonsai he or she will discover new means of accomplishing whatever ends are envisioned.

14. Making Bonsai Containers

FINDING SUBSTITUTES FOR EXPENSIVE ITEMS

It is fun to create your own bonsai tray or pot tailored to your individual ideas but it's unlikely the quality will equal good Chinese and Japanese pots.

The most logical approach to making your own is to decide not to duplicate the imported ones but to create something unique that will complement your trees and accessory plants. For instance, the long, flat trays are expensive, often costing over $100, because of the difficulty of firing such a shape without cracking or warping.

But you can make your own two-or three-compartment trays; long, flat pots designed to hold an island of trees at the center with blue-or green-lined lake compartments for water. Small reeds or dwarf horsetail plants can be planted in the water-tight part of the tray. You might reproduce a scene remembered from long ago or invent a dreamlike ideal scene of a tranquil lake and island (fig. 14–1).

POLYFORM CLAY POTS

There is a plastic modeling compound available at hobby and craft shops called polyform. It can be molded into a pot using armature wire for reinforcement and baked in a home oven. Although not as sturdy as potter's clay it is tough enough to hold its shape, extremely malleable, and can be given any color with acrylic artist's paints. It bakes to a pretty amethyst color. We have used it with greater success for very small-to-medium-size pots and trays. If it rests upon a perfectly flat surface during baking, it will not warp. The clay need not dry before baking. Clear directions are printed on each box. We buy it in 2-pound (about 1 kilogram) boxes, for about $3.95 each.

Knead the clay a few turns, lay it out on a nonporus surface (not polished

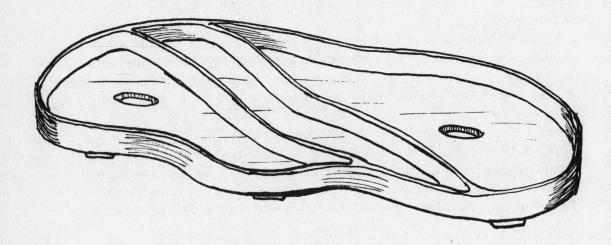

14-1 Your imagination will invent other possibilities—here are a few.

wood, which it may damage); anchor a lathe on each side of the clay mass to keep the sheet perfectly level and roll flat with a large dowel or rolling pin. Cut the bottom and sides to shape and press sides into place. Do not forget drain holes. Apply the feet last. A raised dragon or tree pattern can be contrived by rolling bits of clay and molding them into a design on the sides. A metal nut-pick or an orangewood stick are good tools for pressing clay into place and sculpting incised patterns. Always bake footed trays upside down.

Unless the pot is especially large—over 12–14 inches (31–37 cm)—you will not need reinforcement. Larger shapes can be reinforced with sculpting armature, which is a wire sold in several different sizes for the purpose. Make a flat spiraling coil and sandwich it between two thin layers of clay, pressing and molding them together to avoid air holes. Trim, shape, and proceed as for any pot.

The rustic, free-form tray is easy to make and will turn out at least as good-looking as the commercial type. It is made by pressing lumps of clay around the base to form an irregular edge that will almost disappear when the tray is planted. It looks best colored a dark earth shade.

WOODEN TRAYS

When a really large tray is wanted, wood is lighter in weight than clay and is easier to make at home successfully. Wooden trays can be made with some types of picture-frame stock. Cut a rectangle of marine plywood for the bottom, drill drain holes, nail and glue the mitered frame stock in place, stain, and then preserve the wood with a waterproofing epoxy. If you can't get the picture frame-stock cut to size for you, you will need a miter-box and saw (available from lumber yards or hardware stores), which enables you to cut a perfect 45° angle.

Even oval pots may be made with picture framing. Shape the bottom piece to fit inside the groove of the frame intended for the picture, glue, and completely coat with waterproofing epoxy. Allow the work to dry for a week or more before using it.

SLATE SHEETS

Carpet and tile shops have precut sheets of real slate. The sheet alone can be planted on in the same way as one would use a flat rock, or tree-fern sticks (sold in variety and garden supply stores for training vines into a column) can be glued on for sides. The sticks are easy to cut with a saw or a serrated kitchen knife. There is no need for drain holes since the fern sticks are porous. The effect is very natural and pleasant. The tree roots may invade the moist fern sticks, but come repotting time they will be cut off anyway.

15. General Care

DAILY MAINTENANCE

Daily care is almost as important for bonsai as for a pet cat, dog, or fish. At times when the grower must be absent every care should be taken to see that the trees do not lack for water and protection. But most of the time bonsai should be given personal attention daily.

Making certain the plants do not dry out is of first importance, but this is only one facet of general care. Develop the kind of sensitivity that a mother has for her child; she knows when anything is wrong because she knows so thoroughly how that child looks and behaves when well: Color, activity, manner, response, all give clues when there is some problem.

Growing plants give such signals when something is wrong. The leaves may suddenly seem to droop or curl, or the color or texture is off or not normal for the species. When one is truly familiar with a tree any unexpected change is reason enough to check drainage, exposure, pests, and disease. Look each tree over very carefully and critically each day.

Here are some pointers on general care:

• It's wise to carry small pruners whenever you go out to visit your trees; you may be tempted, as I am, to pinch off that twig that is spoiling the shape of the tree. If you do it by hand you may find that it is too tough and so it hangs there, bruised and wounded. Such messy, haphazard pruning invites disease and looks worse than if it were not done at all. With pruners handy you'll be prepared to nip it off cleanly.

• Clean leaves from the ground cover and bench whenever they fall, not when you have a big cleanup job. Pests and diseases have a better chance if you leave them a place to hide and propagate. Many a problem has been prevented just by clean daily practices.

• Lift the pots frequently—maybe not daily, but often—to look for slugs, sowbugs, angleworms, ants, and any other pests that might hide there. Check also to see that drainage holes are working well. Some pots have such short feet that water tension can hold drainage water under the bottom of the pot for an unhealthy length of time, especially if there are a few leaves, twigs, or dirt particles underneath. Cut away any roots that show; they also will clog drainage.

• Fit plastic aprons over the pots if a rainy spell seems to be keeping soil constantly soggy for too long a time. Prop them up away from the soil surface so that air can circulate. To avoid damaging moss or other ground cover use clear plastic. Only unusually wet weather would prompt this action. If the soil drains properly there is seldom any reason for such concern.

• Observe leaf color and reaction to make sure the sun is not too intense. We find it necessary to change the positions of our trees as the season progresses, moving them to more or less sun according to the appearance of the plant. If the leaves are bigger, softer, and paler than the type should be, give more sun (gradually, of course). If they begin to curl and show brown spots or edges we move to more shade. This last move need not be gradual. Tropicals such as *Ficus* trees will show a whitish, washed-out color on new leaves if they are receiving too much sun. Later brownish patches appear throughout the leaves. Do remember to occasionally turn the trees for even exposure to sun and light.

• Some trees (larch, beech, oak, pine) go into dormancy in the late summer just as heavy rains begin in parts of the country. Protect them from too much water at this time as they can drown if they stay constantly soaked during an inactive, dormant time in the cycle.

• It seems to us that birds show more interest in tearing up moss and mulches at some times of the year than others. If they disturb ground cover you can protect it with an apron or collar of vinyl mesh. Cut a piece big enough to fit over the edge of the pot, slit to the trunk area, cut a circle to fit around the trunk without scuffing it, and fit it over the pot, leaving it there until the little bandits find other pursuits. This cover is also a good sun shade for new moss and helps keep the force of the rain from dislodging it.

• If small pots are in danger of being knocked off the bench by wind, squirrels, or pets, place bricks at strategic positions to brace them or nail small slats of wood around the pot. Be sure you don't make a dam that would interfere with drainage or air circulation.

• Pluck all spent flowers or old fruit immediately; a great deal of strength goes into producing seed which might be better spent in making bigger trunks and new buds.

• Remove old leaves and brown needles. Leaves should be cut, rather than pulled, to avoid damage to new buds. Needles can be pulled off if they come easily.

• Check wires to see that they are not becoming so tight that they cut into the bark.

• Remove any suckers that appear at the base of a tree trunk. Often these suckers take all the nutrients and cause the death of the old trunk.

• Prune out dead twigs. Never leave any of the dead wood when you cut a dead twig or branch; cut to living, healthy tissue, so that it can heal quickly.

• Replace soil that is washed away by careless watering or rain; exposed feeder roots cease to function and look forlorn and messy.

• Watch for dark spots in moss cover, especially if it is unusually luxuriant. This may happen to the loveliest moss and should be immediately picked out. The moss gets these dead spots when there is not enough air circulation so just leave the bare area open for a time. A perfect moss cover without any soil showing is much to be desired but it is wise to regularly pick out a few tiny air holes, just as you would aerate a fine lawn.

• Crusty, scaly mineral salts will collect on the edges of pots. Polish with steel wool, an abrasive scrubbing cloth, or a sponge wet with vinegar water. Baby oil or furniture wax wiped on with a cloth will keep the salts from building up again for some time. Don't oil the entire pot—just the edges where buildup is expected.

• If ants are seen strolling innocently around the area be assured they are not harmless. They bring aphids and scale, carrying them from plant to plant as farmers move cows to new pasture land. The ants then visit their "cows" to milk them of their honeydew. (See Ants, Chapter 16.)

These are some of the things you should have in mind when you take each daily tour of your charges.

WATERING AND THE WORRY-FREE VACATION

Few bonsai growers agree on watering methods. Each will develop methods to suit his or her responsibilities, convenience, region, and micro-climate (the schedule which works on the north side of the house won't work on the south, east or west sides).

Our next-door neighbor doesn't follow my schedule, because even though we both have our trees deployed on the north side of our houses, he has a brick wall extending on the east corner, his house is on higher ground causing rapid drainage of cool air away from his benches, and several large oaks give intermittent shade throughout the day. We have a tall *Juniperus cannaerti* hedge bordering our west yard, our lot is 15 feet (4.4 meters) lower, some of the benches are surrounded by a low privet hedge, and a pool nearby reflects light and stabilizes temperatures. Every feature of your garden influences the growth of your trees so your care schedule will be uniquely your own.

• If a tree needs to be kept constantly moist, the proportion of soil and peat should be a little heavier than standard and it probably should be located in half-shade or dappled sun.

• A tree that should almost dry out between waterings should have more sand or Turface in the mix and should be placed where it gets more sun and wind.

Trees in both the constant-moist and the dry-between-waterings categories can be watered the same amount and at the same times, even though their needs are drastically different, if the above-described soil and exposure considerations are observed.

Huge stone cisterns or troughs filled with water and a beautiful, expensive copper watering can at the ready nearby are a luxury we hope someday to attain, but water straight from the tap is perfectly all right in most parts of the country. The only exceptions might be in the west, where water may have a high alkaline content, or in parts of Florida, where salt water occasionally gets into the water supply. If you have a water softener hooked up to your tap, draw water from a point not affected by it. The salts added by a softener system are deadly to plants.

If you have any doubts about the water, catch rainwater or draw water in large, plastic waste cans or wooden barrels, and allow it to settle three or four days before using. One grower in California whose tapwater is alkaline runs a hose from his kitchen hot-water faucet to fill a large wooden half-barrel. He insists he gets superior results by adding a cup (8 oz. or 240 ml) of white vinegar to each 50 gallons (190 liters) of aged water.

In this case the vinegar is being used to bring the water to a more nearly neutral pH reading but it also is a gentle, useful acidulator to condition water for acid-loving plants. If, for instance, azaleas look chlorotic (with pale green or yellow leaves) they may be receiving water that is too alkaline for their particular systems, preventing them from benefiting from nutrients.

To test the water supply in your area buy an inexpensive pH test kit for $2 or $3 from an aquarium or pet supply store. Don't buy the kind using litmus paper—ask for the kit using bromothymol blue, a liquid chemical. Instructions with the kit make it simple to use. If the water tests 7.8 or more (alkaline) you may want to reduce it to 7.0 neutral or to somewhere between 6.8–6.0 (slightly acid) using the vinegar.

However the water is conditioned the same watering method is followed: Fill the tree's container to the brim several times by flowing the water gently over the soil in such a way that the soil is not washed away. Be sure the soil is completely watered, leaving no dry spots at the center of the soil mass. If there is any doubt submerge the pot to the rim in a container of water until the surface is moist, then lift it out and drain immediately. It's a good practice to do this occasionally with all your trees.

There are perforated nozzles or "roses" made for watering cans which deliver a gentle, fine spray. Nurseries and bonsai supply companies offer a water wand which is fitted with a fine rose that attaches to a hose. These are both very useful. If no rose is used, turn the water pressure very low so that it trickles gently. Water the soil and then rinse the leaves with a spray made by putting your thumb over the nozzle.

Most trees should be watered all over with a soaking for the roots and a good shower to clean and refresh the leaves. There are exceptions: Avoid regular showering of pine needles when they are lengthening in the spring because it makes them over-long. (When needle growth is complete by midsummer, shower regularly.) Also, no tree should have water on its leaves when the sun is shining on it. If there are disease problems such as mildew, rust, or black spot the leaves should be kept dry.

It does no harm to water the soil in full sun. Real damage may result if one waits until the sun is off a tree before watering an obviously dry plant. We often have to water our trees at midday in the blazing sun.

Rock-grown bonsai, tiny *mamé*, and those in very shallow trays need even more careful watering. One can pop out with a watering can four or five times on hot, windy summer days or arrange a drip-watering system which is a boon whether you are at home near your trees all day, at work from nine to five, or on a two-week vacation (fig. 15–1).

Another effective method for trouble-free watering is wicking (fig. 15–2). The pot sits on a reservoir of water and a line or nylon cord is coiled in the bottom of the pot running out the drainage hole into the reservoir. Be sure the line makes a full circle in the bottom of the pot and reaches well down to the bottom of the reservoir. Do not lead the line up the side of the pot. Use nylon cord since cotton, wool, and other natural fibers rot quickly.

To avoid fraying of the ends of the line light a candle and burn the cord rather than cutting it. You can knot it and then cut but it's faster to just burn enough lengths to wick all your pots at one time. A little practice will show you what size to use. One or two strands of fine cord may be adequate for *mamé*, with heavier gauge for larger pots. Once the wick is positioned, the soil actually pulls up the needed amount of water through it.

For a reservoir one can use plastic plant trays from greenhouse supply companies (some good sturdy ones are listed in Park's nursery catalogue) topped with a length of hardware cloth. This arrangement usually holds several pots, which sit on the hardware cloth with their wicks dangling in the water. This way high humidity is maintained around the trees. Separate reservoirs can be contrived from plastic ice cream cartons or small butter tubs with holes cut in the lid—one for the wick and another at one edge for filling and checking water level.

If algae develops dump the water and scrub and rinse the water container. Algae can become so thick it obstructs water flow. To start the wicking action water the plant well. If a plant goes dry refill the reservoir and water the plant—it may not begin to draw properly without this assistance.

For young still-developing plants a constant-feed program can be used. The water is mixed at ¼ strength or less with soluble fertilizer and the plant is fed as it drinks. Watch carefully and adjust the mixture or discontinue it if growth is too long and lank. A standard fertilizing schedule can be followed; just use fertilizer in the water at the usual feeding seasons.

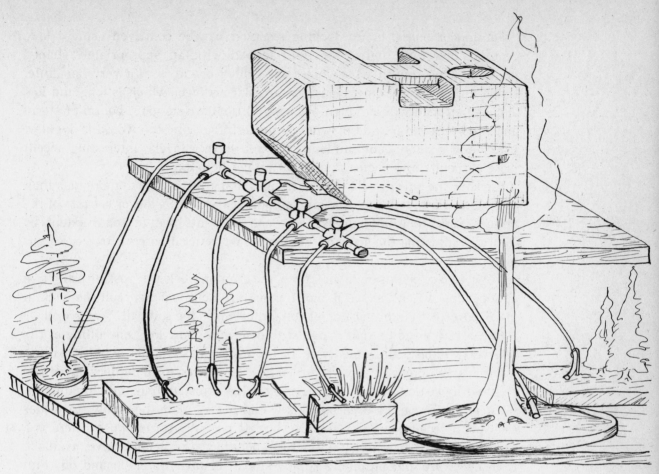

15-1 Reservoir is a plastic spring-water container fitted with small plastic tubing and brass or plastic valves from the aquarium supply shop. Water supply must be above trees, for this is a primitive gravity-flow system. It isn't a thing of beauty, but can easily be concealed. Another reason to hide this system; sunshine causes algae to form, which can interfere with flow of water. Also, plastic tubing could get hot enough to collapse, especially where it bends over the edge of a shelf. Tube outlets should be secured in place with stakes and ties.

15-2 Several small pots wicked and ready for planting. The wick is passed through the drain-hole screen, lying in a coil on the bottom of the pot. It extends well down to the bottom of the reservoir. The pots rest on galvanized hardware cloth, and do not touch the water.

For indoor bonsai a neat-looking reservoir can be contrived using a low, ceramic, flower arranging container topped with an appropriately shaped plastic serving tray in which holes are drilled or cut with a very hot knife. Hylan makes a handsome, black, rectangular arranger which is long and low and about 2 inches (5 cm) high. It looks a little like a standard bonsai platform and is permissible in a decor where a makeshift plastic tub would look out of place. Add a fluorescent Gro-lamp and you have a lovely, interesting accent piece without worry about watering or proper light exposure.

Probably the only drawback to wicking is that growth is often more lush than you might want, with internodes longer and leaves a little bigger because of the unfluctuating moisture supply. This can be controlled to some extent by carefully adjusting the size and number of wicks used on each tree or accent plant.

Any tree can be put on a wick for a vacation or weekend. Just turn the tree out of its pot when the soil is moist enough to hold together, coil the wick in place, cover with a thin sifting of soil, and replace the soil ball. Water well.

Run a test ahead of your vacation to determine how long one filling of the reservoir will last. Allow plenty of reserve water in case of hot, windy weather.

For a large number of trees a garden hose connected to an outdoor tap can be fitted with plastic lines and valves, each valve adjusted to its individual plant. (Mister nozzles can be used but this would not regulate the amount of water each plant receives.) The water can be left partially turned on so there is a constant drip, or an automatic timer can be fitted to a solenoid valve (available from hardware and plumbing supply stores) to turn water on and off. Full instructions come with the kits. (See Chapter 20, Sources.)

Very small containers take a different watering frequency than larger ones so each size should have its own system.

MOISTURE METERS

Almost 7 million moisture meters of one kind of another have been sold and they are being generally well received. People who buy one kind tend to also buy another, whether because of gimmick-fascination or actual appreciation is a matter for conjecture.

Granted, they are interesting. Insert the sensor probe of a moisture meter into distilled water and a "dry" reading registers. Put it on your tongue and the indicator shifts to "wet." You may have guessed by now that the sensor actually gives a salt-level reading! The old scientific principle of electrolysis is employed in the construction of the meters. The probe is made of two kinds of metal with plastic sandwiched between. When moisture, laden with salts from the soil, conducts electricity from metal to metal a reading results.

One danger is that newly fertilized soil will register "wet" even if it is barely damp. Obviously the meters are not exactly accurate but they can be useful if you are not familiar with the needs of a new plant or if you tend to overwater or underwater. If you understand the foibles of the instrument you can use it safely.

Personally we still prefer to adjust the soil mix and light-air exposure of each tree so that little individual attention is needed when watering.

AUTOMATIC WATERING

Eastside Irrigation Service, of Fresno, California, was kind enough to answer some of our questions about automatic watering:

Question: Could a timer be set to run for several minutes at a time twice daily for an indefinite period?

Answer: Our line of electric timers (both indoor and outdoor models) can be set to turn on for from 5–60 minutes one to four times a day. Three different stations can be actuated by one timer, each station having individual settings. By using an extra "watering paddle" the units may be converted so they water automatically up to four times a day at six-hour time periods, then be converted back to once-a-day watering. The timer can also be controlled manually for extra watering or can be turned off in rainy seasons without disrupting the clock movement.

Question: Could the entire system be installed in a greenhouse or on bonsai benches and concealed easily?

Answer: Yes, using $3/16$ distribution tubing, which is flexible and easily hidden.

Question: Would it present any problem if all the bonsai would be located above the water source and at varying levels?

Answer: No, as the system is under 20–30 pounds of pressure. Using this size tubing it is doubtful you would experience a pressure problem.

WINTER CARE

As with all other aspects of bonsai care, winter protection varies with the size of the container, age, species, health of the plant, the climate zone where it naturally thrives, and the climate in which you hope to grow it (fig. 15–3). Other factors are important: Rats, mice, rabbits, and deer may lunch on your precious trees when food becomes scarce; good drainage must be assured; trees must not be left under eaves or gutters where dripping can cause them to be encased in ice. Wind protection is very important. Desiccation (drying) may kill more plants in winter than cold air.

Where winters are fairly severe—zones 3 through 7 and sometimes 8—the basic idea is to keep the plants dormant without allowing any winter injury, such as branch or root dieback or split bark. If dormancy is deep and temperatures remain between 33° and 38° F. (1°-70° C.) deciduous and evergreen plants can be stored where there is no light at all, as in a windowless building or covered pit.

If there is some growth taking place, say at 40° F. (73° C.) and above, evergreens must have light or dieback begins. As long as they are completely leafless deciduous trees do not need light.

In zones 7 and 8, an open shed will protect from frost and wind. If the pots are mulched so that no abrupt temperature changes take place at the root zones, no further protection is necessary. In zones 3, 4, 5, and 6, more careful attention must be given.

An unheated building, garage, or storage shed is a good place for trees to winter. It's necessary to keep soil from drying out too much—otherwise little else is needed. Trees should not be near a south or west window where bright winter sun could encourage premature growth.

For zones 3 and 4 trees in an unheated building should be placed in large boxes filled with sawdust, bark, leaves, or brown peat to cover the soil and reach to the lowest branches. If you have several different-sized bonsai set smaller, shorter pots on the pots of larger trees, then mulch. Guard against rats and mice.

The cold pit is good protection, particularly in zones 3, 4, 5 and 6. A pit about 4 feet (1.2 m) deep is lined with concrete blocks or boards and a 6-inch (15 cm) layer of gravel is spread for drainage. This kind of pit can be any size that is practical but should be at least 4 feet deep. For convenience one might add steps at one side. The bonsai are set in and mulched to the lowest branches. Good drainage is essential, otherwise water from rain or melting snow could drown the whole collection. Use plenty of gravel on the bottom and check during the winter for flooding.

After cold weather settles in (fig. 15-4) and trees are completely dormant a cover is added. An old wooden door or something similar works well. A layer of straw over the cover will keep temperatures constant. Do not install the cover too soon; plants must be completely dormant, weather should be cold, and rodents should be less active by this time. (They move into protected areas if given the opportunity.) Place rodent poison near the trees and scatter moth crystals generously. We don't suggest using Decon or similar substances that actually attract mice. They may smell the inviting aroma and then decide they prefer succulent tree bark instead.

It's usually not necessary to check the trees during the winter unless you are concerned about water. Most often, high humidity keeps moisture loss at a minimum and the collection comes through beautifully.

Average min. temp.
(Fahrenheit)

1 below −50°
2 −50° to −40°
3 −40° to −30°
4 −30° to −20°
5 −20° to −10°
6 −10° to 0°
7 0° to 10°
8 10° to 20°
9 20° to 30°
10 30° to 40°

15–3 Zone map.

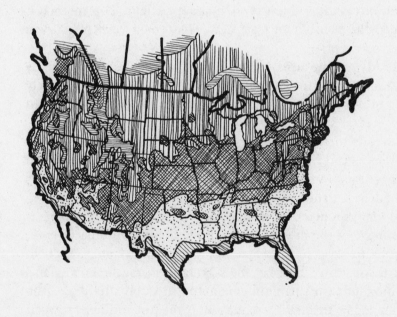

June 30–July 30
July 30–August 30
Aug. 30–Sept. 30
Sept. 30–Oct. 30
Oct. 30–Nov. 30
Nov. 30–Dec. 30

15–4 Average dates of first fall frost.

An insulated attached garage is a fine place for your trees. Even borderline semihardies like crape myrtles, pomegranates, chrysanthemums, catlin elms, some azaleas and other broadleaf evergreens, and other plants hardy in natural or landscape situations in zones 7 and 8 can be wintered here if they are kept above freezing and not allowed to dry out. This detail should be emphasized. We have found the plants we kept in the garage need water at least once weekly.

Smaller trees can be lifted from their pots and temporarily submerged to soil surface level in sand, brown peat, or a rotted sawdust-sand mixture. The medium, which is held in a larger pot or wooden box, is kept damp with fewer waterings than in a pot and there is little temperature fluctuation. There will probably have been some root growth by the plants at repotting time, which shows how well the treatment suits them.

To store a few bonsai without weekly attention, use a frame made of boards and large enough to accommodate them all. Fill with enough mulch to come up level with or slightly above the rims of the pots. Nail together a frame over which clear plastic can be attached in miniature greenhouse fashion. To retain moisture the plastic cover should be close to the tops of the plants but not touching them. Water well. This arrangement should keep them comfortable for several weeks.

This method also works very well for indoor collections. No direct sunlight should be allowed to fall on plastic-covered plants and there should be allowance for some air circulation. Don't try to make it airtight. This method is suggested only to keep the plants moist for a weekend or a week when you won't be at home to tend them.

Bonsai that are hardy to the area where you live can be protected by mulching in. Before and after mulching up to the first branches generously scatter moth crystals to discourage pests. Place the trees in an area protected from the wind, bright winter sunshine, and standing surface water. If trees are located under eaves, be sure dripping water or snow sliding off the roof will not fall on them. Sometimes a gutter will develop a leak just over a valued tree and one day you'll find it encased in ice.

Mulching-in is a fairly satisfactory method but there may be some twig dieback and moss or other ground cover will be partially killed. It helps to place a skirt of vinyl screening over the moss, propped up with a few chunks of bark. Cut a circle of screening to cover to the edges, slit to the center, make a hole to fit very loosely around the trunk, and lay the screening in place. This is also good protection for new moss in springtime, enabling it to breathe under the mulch so it most often comes through undamaged. A retainer wall of firewood or boards can be built to hold the mulch in place.

We have used this method for years. The area chosen is a north-facing garage wall. In summer the bed is luxuriant with hardy ferns which do not protest the trampling in the fall or the mulch, which probably benefits them enormously.

So that spring clean-up is minimal, we use small pine bark, which is deployed around the grounds as spring top-dressing for flower beds. Plants are watered if necessary at this time and further watering is needed only in a very dry winter.

Twig dieback is virtually eliminated with the use of a temporary shelter to keep off frost, but then more care must be given to watering.

The cold greenhouse—with a temperature kept just above freezing—is a wonderful way to protect hardy and semihardy plants. With such a greenhouse, many plants not otherwise practical to keep can be grown. Mosses and other ground covers are not disturbed and tiny bonsai are safe. There is little or no twig dieback. Probably the only drawback is the necessity for frequent watering, which must be done in cold, clammy surroundings. If you take a winter vacation, someone must stand in for you.

If you build a cold greenhouse be sure to install an automatic ventilating system. Without a ventilator system you may end up with over-cooked plants, or, at the very least, winter sun can overheat the greenhouse so that some plants begin to grow only to be shocked by the return of colder weather. The ventilator has louvers that open when the air reaches a preset temperature and close again automatically. The system is not cheap, but when you go to the expense of a greenhouse, it should be built properly.

Bonsai growing in a city apartment is complicated by a lack of appropriate wintering facilities. If you have a balcony you can build a brick and board bench (see Chapter 17, Benches). During the summer use it to display your bonsai then store them under the bench in the winter. Under these benches a thermostatically controlled heat cord (of the type used for heating cold frames) can be laid on the floor of the deck or balcony, held in place and away from the trees with a few bricks. The trees are placed under the bench as soon as cold weather is well under way and burlap or plastic sides are nailed to the edges of the shelves and weighted down securely with bricks. If plastic is used be sure it is at least 3 millimeters thick so that the wind will not whip and tear it. Leave air circulation spaces at the top and bottom. One of the advantages of using burlap is that it allows a good air exchange, without airholes. The soil should remain barely moist; it won't be necessary to water often.

The heat cord is not intended to keep the plants warm but to hold the temperature slightly above freezing. In fact, it is not necessary in most of our climate zones if the trees are hardy. In zones 2 through 5 it's a good safety measure, however, especially if the balcony is on a second story or above.

TROPICALS AND SEMITROPICALS

Plants hardy only to zones 9 and 10 are tropicals and semitropicals which must be kept in good growing conditions throughout the year. They do have inactive periods but they resent temperatures below 50–55° F. (approx. 18–

23° C.). For these, a sunny window sill, sun room, or even a warm greenhouse could serve but a very good solution is an artificial light arrangement. Properly planned and executed, this is an excellent way to maintain plants whether just for the winter or year around.

In zones 2 through 6 or 7 there are weeks on end in winter when there just isn't enough natural light to support good compact growth. When artificial light is used either to supplement natural light or completely fill the light needs of our plants we can enjoy watching them progress nicely all year whether we live in the south or the north!

ARTIFICIAL-LIGHT GARDENING

This is a whole new field with many delightful side-benefits. It is unequalled for *mamé*, giving ideal growing conditions under almost perfect protection. Rock-grown bonsai that are difficult to winter in mulch bed or garage, multilevel terrains in shallow trays, and many other special-care bonsai take very well to artificial-light gardening (fig. 15–5). Trays of moss can be grown, ready for spring repotting (see Accent Plants and Ground Covers, Chapter 9). Blooming accent plants, tiny trays of grasses, and bog plants can be always at hand.

Nearly any plant considered tropical or semitropical can be expected to thrive under artificial light and many others not necessarily tropical respond vigorously. Some, which require a period of cold, can serve a term in the insulated garage then be brought in to resume growing.

Ivies, *Ficus*, catlin and Hokaido elms, wild thyme azaleas (this is one that requires a term of cold), junipers, *chamaecyparis*, boxwoods, broad-leaf hollies, miniature orchids, camellias, *carissa, serissa, malpighia*, red mangrove, and *cryptomeria* are only a few of the plants we have found to grow very successfully under artificial light. Cascade styles must be laid on their backs (righted only for watering) unless you install a few vertical fluorescent tubes on a nearby wall.

Any area can be adapted to fluorescent light gardening providing the temperature ranges between 55–80° F. (23–48° C.). A converted closet, space under a stairway, bookshelves, an empty fireplace, the under-cabinet space of a kitchen counter, or—my favorite—a corner of the basement.

One grower banished both cars to the driveway and converted the entire garage. Another decided a dining room was completely unnecessary and made it into a fairyland of tropical bonsai. She has at least two of each species, one to grow as bonsai and the other, of the same age and variety, to grow unpruned and untrained in a large pot. It makes a fascinating test-and-compare garden.

She follows the same precept with her outdoor plants, with 30-foot (9 m) birches towering over their same-age 18-inch (50 cm) siblings nearby, and 8-foot (2.4 m) quince bushes flanking 10-inch (25 cm) sisters.

The ideal artificial-light garden has walls and ceiling painted flat white. No other surface, not even a mirror, reflects as much energy. Each light unit contains two to four 48-inch (125 cm) tubes installed in a reflector that can be lowered or raised on counterweights. The inside of the reflector should be flat white. The plants rest on galvanized hardware cloth over sturdy plastic trays of peat or vermiculite, which is kept damp. The trays can be filled with a weak fertilizer solution instead of just plain water and wicks leading from pot to tray can provide for constant-feed culture (see Chapter 15, Watering and the Worry-Free Vacation). The pot bottoms should not touch the vermiculite, which might cause an invasion of pests.

15–5 Fluorescent light gardening can be combined with window bonsai growing. These indoor bonsai are more decorative than bric-a-brac or drapes! The shelves can be fitted with the new stick-in-place tubes or conventional ones installed by an electrician. Don't depend upon Gro-lights for reading; our eyes can't really see well with them.

We have tested many kinds of fluorescent tubes, finding that plants will grow under any of them. In our opinion, the very best choice is Gro Lux, by Sylvania. Plant-Gro, by Westinghouse, is also very good but not as easy to come by in our area so we haven't used the light as much. Because we have found the Gro Lux system satisfactory, we haven't investigated the use of incandescent lighting, either as a supplement or as the complete system.

Since Gro Lux lights compel vigorous growth the plants are fed as if they were at the peak growing period of late spring, which this system simulates. Many of our little trees are on a constant-feed system, getting a liquid solution at ⅛ to ¼ strength—that is, ¼ teaspoon soluble fertilizer to each gallon of water—with each watering. Occasionally they are submerged in a clear water bath to flush mineral salts away.

This ideal light system has an inexpensive, automatic electric timer that assures 16 hours of light. And since fluorescent tubes use less than ⅕ the energy of incandescent bulbs, the cost of a 16-hour day for two 40-watt tubes will be around 7 cents a day in our area. The cost varies a little with each utility company. Industrial fluorescent light reflectors can be bought ready to hang and plug in or you can have an electrician install them directly under the plant shelves.

Wash tubes regularly for dust or mineral deposits from misting plants cut down on the amount of energy transmitted to the trees. Since the tubes don't get hot, you need not worry about water causing a bulb to break. We've never used ice-cold water for washing or misting but we have never experienced breakage with room-temperature water. Fluorescent tubes lose efficiency as they age. Replace them when you see dark rings at the ends or when they are 18-20 months old, whichever comes first.

Plants requiring the strongest light should be placed nearest the tubes and can actually touch them without burning. Those normally growing in shade can be positioned at the ends of the tubes where there is less light emission. Only experimentation can tell you how far to place a plant from the lights. Some need strong light, almost touching. As they grow they can be moved a little further away. Some trees and accent plants can be as much as 18 inches (45 cm) from the light source. If the growth is green and compact, the distance is right. Spindly, pale, upreaching leaves tell you stronger, closer light is needed. As the tubes weaken with age, plants can be moved closer.

We make use of every square inch by installing cup hooks on the underside of the shelf beside the tubes and hang the smallest bonsai in that space which would otherwise be empty.

An unexpected bonus becomes manifest when you first see plants under Gro Lux lamps. The colors are vivid—vibrant beyond any description: Pinks and reds glow, yellows and whites sparkle, blues are intense, and all leaf-greens are lively. You'll probably be adding new light units as soon as the first ones have demonstrated the benefits of this newest mode of gardening.

16. Pests, Diseases, Deficiencies

PREVENTION

Prevention of disease is more important than cure for once a disease organism invades its host it is a difficult matter to remove it and undo its effects. For all our study and experimentation, we know little about curing disease.

Probably the very best preventive measures are cleanliness, good feeding and maintenance practices, and the obliteration of insect invaders, who may leave spores of rust, mildew, and blight wherever their little feet touch. Wind, water, and contaminated tools also contribute to the spread of disease, but insects are the principal offenders.

A strong, clean, well-groomed plant is unlikely to fall victim to serious disease unless it is far from its natural home or has suffered a trauma, such as might come about if it is moved from one exposure to another.

In addition to the preventive measures already mentioned you can use a weekly all-purpose insecticide spray. If there are indications of mildew or rust a fungicide such as benomyl will clear it up. Just rinsing the entire tree at the time of each watering can discourage pests. A shower of liquid detergent—1 teaspoon (5 ml) of Palmolive or a like product to 1 quart (.95 l) of water—sprayed on and rinsed off will dispatch many insect pests such as scale, mealy bugs, spider mites, and aphids. Small bonsai can be dipped in the solution.

Learn to distinguish mechanical damage and soil deficiencies from disease. Otherwise you may be giving a plant medicine when the real need is for some environmental or physiological adjustment.

NUTRITION DEFICIENCIES

Symptom	Soil Type Most Often Affected	Remedy
Dark green leaves of spring become grayish, with seared tips and edges	Sandy	Potash
Leaves assume purplish margins; growth is stunted; flowering is sparse or nonexistent	Very acid	Phosphorus, traces of iron, potash
New leaves deformed, with yellow edges	Very acid	Calcium, potash, with traces of manganese and iron. Reduce acidity slowly with gypsum.
Leaves all gradually become yellow with green veins—commonly affects azalea, ivy	Sandy	Nitrogen
Older leaves yellow first, leaving green veins	Sandy	Magnesium, potash. Spray with Epsom salts.
New leaves turn yellow-green, with green veins—commonly affects fruit trees, azaleas	Peaty or sandy soils	Spray plant and soil with iron chelate.
Leaves have irregular yellow blotches; veins are very dark-green color	Sandy	Zinc, manganese

Symptom	Soil Type Most Often Affected	Remedy
Tips of branches wilt and die—usually after a long rainy spell	Sandy	Copper

MECHANICAL AND OTHER DAMAGE

Symptom	Cause	Remedy
Dry, curled leaves with brown edges	Too strong wind and/or sun	Locate in more protected positon.
Leaves look whitish then develop dark blotches—*Ficus* and other tropicals most often affected	Sun too strong—often seen on trees suddenly moved to sunnier location	Never suddenly move any plant into a sunnier location.
Bark splits lengthwise and stands away from tree	May happen when a heavily foliaged tree is pruned, or when bright winter sun shines on frozen bark.	Place a lath or bit of screening over any bark that is suddenly exposed. Protect from bright sun in winter.
Shredded leaves—no apparent insects	Damage by birds, dogs, cats	Birds: Use screening, or bright windmills and wind chimes. Dogs, cats: try offering some grassy sod placed in a flat nearby.
Newly opened leaves are distorted by crimps; brown lines may be present	Injury to new buds	Be sure buds are not handled or bumped. Remove distorted leaves.

Symptom	Cause	Remedy
Bark is blotched, is smoother and flatter than normal in irregular areas, and may also be lighter in color	Pressure of hands or tools used at some time in the past	Avoid allowing anything to press or lean against trunk or branches.
Bark stands away at edges of pruning wound	Heavy pruning at season of fast growth	Prune only when growth is slow—best time is before seasonal growth spurts begin.
Leaves of broad-leaved evergreens develop pattern of fine crackling—may turn brown and drop off—occasionally fatal	Use of insecticides incompatible with plant species	No cure. Examine warnings and instructions on all insecticide labels before use.
Abraded, chewed spots—most often happens in winter	Rodents	Deploy moth repellent crystals generously. Poison or trap offenders. Hav-a-hart makes traps that do not injure animals, which may be transferred elsewhere.
Round, brown spots on leaves	Hot sun makes water droplets act as burning-glass on leaves.	Never allow water on leaves while sun is shining on them.
Crinkled, brown leaf edges and/or tips	Low humidity or too much handling, crowding, traffic	Mist frequently. Raise humidity by placing plants on pebble trays with water not quite covering pebbles—do not allow plants to sit in water. Move plants out of traffic areas.

Symptom	Cause	Remedy
Buds form, but drop off before opening	Low humidity, sudden change in atmosphere, as when a plant is moved from greenhouse to home	Anticipate this possibility and mist plant frequently with tepid water.

DISEASES

Symptom	Cause	Remedy
Gray white dusting on leaves and stems; leaves may become distorted	Mildew (fungi)	Spray with benemyl (Benlate).
Growth stunted; leaves are mottled and crinkled	Mosaic (virus)	Cut and burn infected parts, remove and burn any fallen leaves.
Foliage is deformed with concentric spots	Ring Spot (virus)	Same as above
Yellowish discoloration in spots; black spots surrounded by reddish areas inside the yellow discolorations—apple family and quince family are commonly affected	Rusts (fungi)	Junipers are the culture host and rusts cannot propagate without them. Spray junipers with wettable sulphur in early spring—apples and quince with Actidione several times in spring and early summer.
Brownish-gray furry spots on leaves—not as powdery looking as mildew	Botrytis (fungi)	Move to less humid area. Spray with benemyl (Benlate).

Symptom	Cause	Remedy
Branch wilts then leaves shrivel and die— elms and oaks most often affected	Wilt (Dutch elm disease, oak wilt)	There are many types of wilt, all difficult or impossible to treat. Prune out wilted branches, disinfect wounds with alcohol. Keep insects away. Disinfect tools with alcohol.
Pine needles from previous year develop small yellow spots in spring which enlarge and become bands around the needles— needles yellow completely and drop off	Needle-cast (fungus)	Leaves infected the previous year should be plucked and burned (only when they are dry). Spray tree with maneb at two-week intervals, starting in midsummer. For best dates to spray in your area, contact your county agricultural extension agent.
Leaves develop black spots which eventually fall out, leaving open holes—many kinds of plants are subject to such leaf-spots	Black leaf-spot—Some caused by bacteria, some by fungus	Remove and burn all infected leaves. Keep leaves dry. Improve air circulation. Spray with ferbam, nabam.
Pine needles show yellow or yellowish-brown spots— after several months bark yellows and oozes a yellowish liquid, branches die and branch ties hang like red-brown tassels	White pine blister rust (fungus)	Prune affected branches and paint wound with Actidione BR. Gooseberry/currant family is alternate host without which this disease can't survive— will not spread from pine to pine. Disinfect tools used.

Symptom	Cause	Remedy
Maple leaves look as if spattered with tar—not usually serious but disfiguring	Maple tar spot (fungi)	Destroy all affected leaves. Spray with Bordeaux mixture. Follow all cautions on spray.
Azalea leaves swell until monstrously deformed	Azalea leaf gall	Not serious but very ugly. Remove and destroy all deformed leaves.

INSECTICIDES

Organic insecticides are the oldest and the newest kinds. They were the first to be used, and now that people are becoming conscious of the danger of the synthetic varieties, organics are receiving new appreciation. Pyrethrum, made from several of the chrysanthemum species, is popularly used on a wide range of insects. Rotonone, another plant derivative that acts both as contact and stomach poison, is especially effective for caterpillars. Nicotine sulfate, derived from tobacco, is dangerous to vertebrates but is a most effective remedy for most soft-bodied insects, especially aphids. It is used also in its natural dried form as a fumigant. We can personally testify to its effectiveness in this respect—ever been in a smoke-filled room?

Inorganic contact insecticides (sulphur dusts, lime and sulphur, sulphur compounds) are useful against mites and scale insects in their crawling stage. Bordeaux mixture, a combination of copper sulphate and lime, is effective against fungus, but we usually prefer the convenient benemyl. Use all sulphur compounds at a little less than recommended strength and always when temperatures will remain below 80° F. (28° C.) for 24 hours. Chlordane, dieldrin, heptichlor, and aldrin are chlorinated hydrocarbons. They are useful for soil insects, including ants, sowbugs, angleworms (earthworms), and grubs. Malathion, an organo-phosphate, combats a wide spectrum of insects and is not as dangerous as others of its family.

Properly timed and applied, oils destroy scales, mites, some larvae, insect eggs, and aphids. Their main action is to smother creatures which breathe through their skins. Dormant oils are sprayed on leafless trees; they are too heavy to use when leaves are present. Summer or white oils are lighter and can be used—with caution—during the growing season. Follow mixing and application instructions exactly or they might injure plants or fail to accomplish their purpose.

You can expect general insect control if the product combines two or three of these ingredients: Methoxychlor, D.D.T., Diazinon, lindane, chlordane, or malathion.

IDENTIFYING AND CONTROLLING INSECTS

Learning to identify and classify pests is the first step in controlling them. Once you know whether you are dealing with a chewing insect or a sucking insect, you'll know better what measures to take.

For chewing insects, which leave holes in leaves, you can use a stomach poison such as the arsenic compounds or some fluorine compounds, like sodium fluoaluminate. There are many other stomach poisons sold under various trade names. All are dangerous to vertebrates—that's you and me, our children, pets, and birds! They should be stored and handled with great respect. Read and follow instructions.

Sucking pests are combated with contact insecticides, which are also dangerous. Since many of these are fumigants, do not open the package until you have read all instructions. Keep all insecticides clearly marked POISON far from children and pets. Contact insecticides are designed to kill when sprayed or dusted on the bodies of pests. They are often applied to surfaces where insects will encounter and absorb the poison.

Some of these contact poisons as well as some of the systemics (which are absorbed into the plant's system and poison insects that attack it) are dangerous to certain plants. Most labels list which plants can and cannot tolerate the insecticide.

It's important to recognize signs that betray the presence of insects or disease so we'll acquaint you with a few of the most common insect pests.

APHIDS

Aphids are usually seen in early spring. They are soft-bodied bugs, pinhead-size or smaller. Clustering thickly on new growth, they suck juices from and transmit viral diseases to plants. They may be reddish, black, brown, or a pretty shade of green. The males are winged. Give the plant a bath with detergent or spray or with nicotine sulphate or rotonone.

ANTS

These wasp-waisted insects have admirable community organization, but one of their accomplishments—livestock farming—condemns them as pests.

They transport aphids from one plant to another, tending them carefully and milking them for the honeydew exuded when the ants stroke the aphid's body. Use chlordane or heptachlor against ants.

WORMS

Angleworms (earthworms) tunnel in the soil. They may be seen struggling frantically to the surface and are most often seen when the soil is saturated. They also appear at drainholes of plant pots after you give the pot a good rap with a stick. Their castings (excrement) appear on the soil surface in little piles. They channel the flow of water so that it may run out the bottom before soaking into the soil. Use chlordane against them.

Bagworms are caterpillars that feast upon trees and other plants, building a bodycase of webbing and plant debris as they go. Pluck them off and destroy, or spray with any broad-spectrum insecticide or use a systemic. Read the insecticide label to make sure the plants you intend to spray can tolerate the chemical you are using.

BEETLES

These chewing insects take many forms but they and their larvae have one distinctive feature—chewing mouthparts. Usually they can be picked off the plant and destroyed by hand or use any stomach poison.

BORERS

Borers of many kinds attack ginkgo, fruit and flowering trees, birches, and a host of other plants. Prevention is very important; an early spring spraying of dieldrin or malathion, repeated at two-week intervals all summer, may help. Keep debris away from tree trunks. In early fall, paradichlorobenzine crystals can be spread in a ring around a tree 2 or 3 inches away and covered with soil. However, if borers are prevalent they probably will invade your fruit trees. Watch for sawdust on the trunk, branches, or soil, or for clear gum-like clots on the bark. Probe with a wire, dig out the varmints with a sharp knife, or inject nicotine paste or carbon bisulphide into the tunnels and plug with wax or clay. Since the borers tend to clog their tunnels with gum or excrement at intervals they are difficult to eradicate in this way, but try anyway. If left unchecked they will almost certainly kill the tree.

CATERPILLARS

Caterpillars eat leaves and by day they can usually be found hiding under a leaf, rolled up in a leaf, or under a clod of soil. Give them the same treatment as beetles.

CUTWORMS

These dull gray worms are death to tiny seedlings. They hide in the soil and cut seedling stems at night. Chlordane or Diazinon should get rid of them.

LEAFHOPPERS

Streamlined little insects that hop at the slightest disturbance, leafhoppers suck plant juices and transmit viral diseases from plant to plant. They also bite humans, and an interesting but unsubstantiated theory has been advanced to the effect that leafhoppers might possibly infect humans with some plant diseases.

MEALYBUGS

Mealybugs are easy to spot; they are cottony-looking sucking insects. Use a mixture of rubbing alcohol and water (half of each) to dab on their bodies with cotton swabs. If they return use a detergent bath, or white oil emulsion can be sprayed on the affected plants when temperatures can be expected to stay between 30 and 80 degrees F. for three or four days. Malathion or Diazinon can be used any time. If you must spray indoor plants at a time when they cannot be set outdoors for the treatment use malathion, closely adhering to package directions, or use a detergent wash followed by a good rinse. Repeat treatment may be necessary.

Occasionally soil mealy bugs attack house plants and injure roots to such an extent that they cannot function. Most often a few can be seen at the base of the plant and if you turn over moss or soil you will see more. If a plant does not respond to watering or wilts unexpectedly investigate the roots. A good drenching with chlordane or malathion will eradicate them.

PLANT LICE

Psillids are very active, springing plant lice. Spray them with malathion.

MITES

Red spider mites may be present if leaves or needles begin to turn a yellowish green or take on a rusty appearance. Test for mites by shaking a branch over white paper and looking for very tiny moving specks. Fine webbing also may be seen on the needles or leaves. Junipers are a species that is often attacked. Use a Palmolive bath, Aramite, or Dimite. You may never encounter mites if trees are sprayed with water frequently and forcefully since mites cannot stand being wet.

SAWFLIES

Sawflies are fiendishly clever at camouflage. You will detect their work before you see them—disguised as pine needles. Early in the season their feeding causes old needles to deform and yellow. Use malathion or D.D.T.—if you can get it—very early in spring. Repeat a month later and again in August.

GNATS

Soil fungus gnats look like tiny black gnats flying around a few inches above the soil. Their larvae feed on root tips. Use chlordane against them.

SCALES

These are sucking bugs that cover themselves with a waxy coating. They are not easy to see but betray their presence by exuding honeydew, which shows up as sticky, shiny spots on the leaves. There are many sizes, shapes and colors, but the most common are of pinhead or slightly larger size and appear as smooth brown bumps on stems or the upper and lower surfaces of leaves. Found on most kinds of plants they can be white, black, red, or brown. They may be shaped like a grain of rice (euonymous scale, Japanese wax scale), large black half-spheres (hibiscus scale), brown and irregular (citrus scale, oyster scale), white and talcum-like (holly tea scale, cottony maple scale), or almost microscopic size (Ficus scale). Some types reside on the undersides of the leaves only and inadvertently announce their activities by making a whitish spot on the upper surface. Treat as for mealy bugs.

SLUGS, SNAILS

Use snail bait on these and clean away all hiding places such as bits of wood, leaves, or other debris. Slugs and snails chew up leaves and flowers and their damage resembles caterpillar depredation. You can trap them with half an empty grapefruit rind placed cut side down. Lift and clean it every morning. Slugs and snails also are attracted to beer in which they willingly drown. A low saucer of it, with the soil pulled up around for easy access, will dispose of many of them.

THRIPS, OAT LICE

These are tiny, slender insects that attack flowers, leaves, and stems, rasping away the tissues and leaving the plants looking seared and brown. Flowers may fail to open fully, and white, dry stripes may appear on strap-leaved plants. Thrips are difficult to see. Lindane or dieldrin can be used against them.

SOWBUGS, PILLBUGS

Sowbugs and pillbugs act like miniature armadillos, which roll themselves into perfectly round balls when startled. As youngsters we called them roly-polies. They eat root hairs and may become very numerous in a short time, congregating in moist, protected areas under pots and debris. Use chlordane, Diazinon, or snail bait.

WHITE FLIES

These tiny, pristine-white, fly-like insects rise up in a cloud when their hiding places under leaves are disturbed. They suck plant juices and transmit viral diseases. Use Malathion, repeated at two-week intervals until no further infestation is evident.

17. Benches

Bonsai look charming scattered about the garden, terrace, or balcony. A plant can be set upon a stack of bricks, ornamental cinder blocks, an upended log, or on a retaining wall. But to lend an air of stability and importance nothing equals a special bench, whether to hold a single tree or a collection (figs. 17-1—5).

In our garden we use all the above mentioned stands but our favorites are the benches. They can be made of wood (redwood, western cedar) or brick and board, which can be dismantled for winter storage. Some benches have been so planned that they furnish the framework for a wintering-shed with plastic or burlap walls.

A BRICK-AND-BOARD BENCH

This plan can be used for any terrace and looks especially handsome on an apartment balcony, where there are seldom any architectural features that suggest a garden. Make three or more stacks of bricks, depending upon the length and thickness of the board to be laid on top and the amount of weight it will carry. Set the stacks a few inches from the wall and use this as a top level for the smaller pots. Do not underestimate the weight of a potted plant or bonsai; lifting them one at a time may not impress you, but weight adds up. Boards will eventually sag unattractively under the weight if the spaces between supports are too great. Estimate the space your trees will need so that branches will not be cramped. For the second and lower rank start the racks about a foot in front of the first one. Make the second set of supports shorter, stair-stepping the arrangement. If there is room the lower board should be a little wider than the top one; you'll always need as much growing area as you can manage, and bonsai look and grow better if given good air circulation.

These benches can be easily adapted for winter storage of your bonsai (see Chapter 15, Winter Care).

17-1, 2 This sturdy bench complements a large bonsai. It was constructed of western cedar. The 6 × 6 foot legs were sawed and chiseled to fit over the recessed top, making a simple and striking design.

17-3 Another version of the same idea; this time the top sets into recesses formed in the square legs.

17-4, 5 Not really a garden bench for cats and people, it holds small bonsai. Note hand-hewn timbers for look of rugged stability. *(Designed and made by Dale Dunton.)*

18. Potting and Exhibiting Areas

SHOWING YOUR BONSAI

There are almost endless ways of exhibiting bonsai, indoors and out, which can be adapted to your available space and the size of your collection. You can use bookcases, tables, counters, and windows for the indoor trees. In the patio or garden you can show bonsai on tables, benches and walls, or build a shelter for them. You can devote just one area to showing them or design the garden itself to complement your art (figs. 18-1—15). In all cases, however, try to locate your work and storage place as close as possible to the display area.

REDWOOD

Knowing a few simple facts about redwood lumber, which is the best for this purpose, will help you get the best performance from a garden structure at the most economical cost. Selecting the right grade is one of the most important steps.

GARDEN GRADES

Use only a heartwood grade of redwood (Select Heart, Construction Heart, or Clear All Heart) for posts, groundhugging skirtboards, and any framework that comes within 6 inches of the ground or where the wood will come into contact with soil and alternate cycles of wetting and drying. Natural chemicals in the reddish-brown heartwood are resistant to decay and insect attack. For other structural members grades of redwood containing cream-colored sapwood (Select, Construction Common, and Clear) are not only structurally sound but visually very attractive. Clear redwood and redwood plywood provide greater weather tightness for garden shelter storage units.

The garden grades of redwood, which contain knots and are usually more highly figured and patterned than the top grades, offer redwood's unique natural beauty and workability at a lower cost, and their characteristically natural look and texture make them ideal for garden shelters.

Construction Heart: Contains knots up to approximately one third of the width of the piece and allows some manufacturing imperfections if they do not cause waste.
Construction Common; Similar to Construction Heart except that sapwood is permitted.
Merchantable; Contains larger knots and more imperfections than the other garden grades. Loose knots and knotholes occur in some pieces. This grade can be recut economically for many uses.

Construction Common and Merchantable may contain any amount of sapwood including some all-sapwood pieces.

CARE AND HANDLING

Take good care of the lumber between the time it is delivered and actually put to use. Store the lumber flat, under cover, off the ground, and where the wood won't get walked on, banged into, or otherwise scarred. Lumber that sags in storage or is leaned against a wall may warp or bend permanently.

GRAIN AND TEXTURE

Depending on the cut of the millsaw, boards may have a vertical grain, which shows as parallel grain lines on the board face or as a flat grain with marbled figures. Flat grain boards should be placed bark side up to minimize raised grain and splinters. This is especially important for seating, hand rails, and similar surfaces. To determine the bark side of flat grain lumber look at the end of the piece. When the bark side is face up the annual growth rings are arched upwards like the top segment of a rainbow.

You have to exercise judgment when working with boards containing knots. In load-bearing applications large knots should be placed over joists or other supports. This may mean laying the boards loosely on a trial basis to check the best arrangement of pieces.

Redwood lumber can be rough, smooth-surfaced, or resawn, depending on the effect desired. Surfaced lumber emphasizes redwood's grain and color. Rough and resawn (saw-textured) redwood weathers exceptionally well and penetrating finishes last up to twice as long as on surfaced wood.

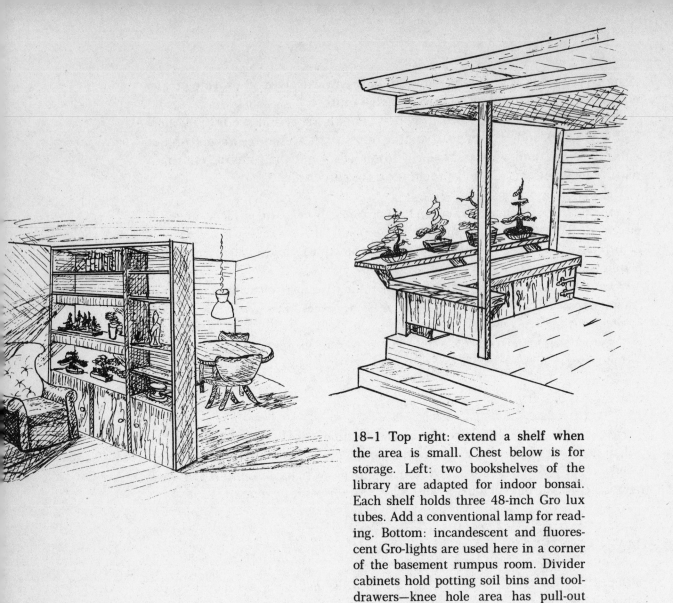

18–1 Top right: extend a shelf when the area is small. Chest below is for storage. Left: two bookshelves of the library are adapted for indoor bonsai. Each shelf holds three 48-inch Gro lux tubes. Add a conventional lamp for reading. Bottom: incandescent and fluorescent Gro-lights are used here in a corner of the basement rumpus room. Divider cabinets hold potting soil bins and tool-drawers—knee hole area has pull-out shelf for repotting.

18-2 The new greenhouse window is offered in several sizes and prices.

18-3 Add extra steps to retainer walls for bonsai display.

18-4 A thick slice of log
stands in the mint bed to
support a Japanese maple.

18-5 Thread-leaf maple on the
terrace table.

18-6 This is why it's called
thread-leaf!

18-7 It's wise to fence your bonsai garden.

18-8 A small part of the Ann Pipe collection. They are kept in this lath house during the summer.

18-9 Ann's trident maple grove in the foreground, Chinese elm grove to the right. The large tree on the left is a Ginkgo, imported from Japan many years ago.

18-10, 11 (*Ann Pipe collection*)

18-12 Bonsai pruning techniques can be applied to pines in the landscape for special effects.

18-13 A dramatic setting for an old pine.
(Dale Dunton garden design)

187

18-14 Shade trellis with redwood slats.

18-15 A lovely garden gate.

FINISHES

Redwood, because of its durability and weather resistance, offers more freedom in selecting a finish than most other exterior building materials.

Water Repellent: A water repellent retards natural weathering, reduces the effects of moisture, and protects the wood from dirt and grime. It can serve as a finish in itself or as an undercoat for further finishes such as a bleach or stain. (Wait at least two weeks before staining.) If no other finish is used a second application of water repellent is recommended six months after the first. Water repellent will modify the natural weathering process, eliminating the dark initial stage, and will help to stabilize the color at a buckskin tan. It is necessary to reapply a water repellent every two to three years. Be sure to follow manufacturer's directions carefully and read the warnings on the label.

Bleach: Application of a wood bleach will hasten the driftwood gray effect achieved through natural weathering.

Pigmented Stains: This type of finish can be used to obtain special color effects. Semitransparent stains do not completely obscure the grain and texture of the wood and thus provide a more natural appearance than opaque stains or paint.

Paint: Exterior wood paints are durable and are available in a wide variety of colors. Paints are not recommended, however, for use on unseasoned lumber. If paint is used a good quality oil-based primer should be applied first.

Varnishes: Do not use varnish or other clear, film-forming finishes on exterior wood surfaces as this type of finish deteriorates rapidly when exposed to sunlight and water.

NAILS AND FASTENINGS

Use only top quality, hot-dipped, galvanized, aluminum alloy or stainless steel nails and other fastenings. Noncorrosive nails and fastenings should always be used outdoors. The slight additional cost of noncorrosive nails is justified by superior performance. Any type of metal not galvanized by the hot-dip process will corrode when exposed to moisture and stain the wood with hard-to-remove streaks, and will cause nails and screws to loose their holding power. (This information is courtesy of the California Redwood Association, 617 Montgomery St., San Francisco, California 94111.)

GARDEN SHELTERS

Some considerations for planning a redwood garden shelter:

REGULATIONS

Check your local building authorities regarding codes, permits, fees.

SITE PLAN

Draw a plan of your property, preferably to scale, showing structures, plantings, walks, etc.

USE

Location and design are determined by use. You may want to think of uses according to generations: Adults will probably use the shelter for such purposes as relaxing, outdoor dining, gardening, entertaining; and children for a sleeping bag bunkhouse, playhouse, playpen, and uses depending on their ages (figs. 18–16, 17).

STORAGE

Allow ample storage space for both general use and specific items, especially larger ones. Adjustable shelves for smaller items offer greater adaptability of storage space (figs. 18–18, 19).

LANDSCAPE

Relationship of the shelter to neighboring structures, landscaping, and general scenery is all-important. A shelter can screen off an inferior view or service area, focus attention on a pleasant vista, and/or act as a focal point of the garden or lawn.

TOPOGRAPHY

Sloping sites sometimes require more intricate construction, but they may also offer more scenic views and added design interest. On a level site a multilevel shelter can achieve the same two goals. A shelter floor flush with the ground means fewer steps, can be a great convenience to the elderly or handicapped.

18–16, 17 Garden shelter perfectly suited for bonsai display.

191

18-18 Back is work area.   18-19 Neat as a pin when all closed up.

192

FLOORING

A redwood deck makes a fast-draining, easily maintained floor and can extend the limits of the shelter.

PRIVACY

Orient the shelter away from too-close neighbors and for maximum privacy from street noise, traffic, and passersby on the sidewalks. Protect your storage area with some locked spaces. Perhaps the entire structure can be designed to be closed up during long, unused periods.

NATURE

Take into account the direction of prevailing breezes and the sun's path throughout the year. Most shelters have at least one wall, either solid or louvered, for protection against the weather. A line of cabinets and shelves can also perform this function. The amount of sun and rain received in your area will determine whether you need an open or solid roof or a combination of both. Sliding solid panels or removable sections of lattice offer light protection against the weather and allow for seasonal adjustments. A lath or slat roof of redwood creates shadows while letting light penetrate and breaks the wind without stopping vertical air circulation.

UTILITIES

You may want a telephone extension or an outside bell installed in your pavilion. Some shelters are almost second homes with running water, electricity, and plumbing. The more independent the shelter, the further it can be from the house; otherwise, carefully consider how far it will be necessary to carry things.

DESIGN

Most shelters are essentially rectangular, but variations are possible using the same basic construction elements. Where a more intricate design, such as an hexagonal, is contemplated, it is wise to seek professional assistance. Flat and sloping shed roofs are by far the most commonly employed in garden shelter design. Gable and pyramid roofs are somewhat more complicated for the do-it-yourselfer to undertake, but they are basic roof designs and most building contracters can handle them with ease (figs. 18–20—23).

You may find that an adaptation of a redwood shelter you have seen fits your requirements exactly, or you may want to design one yourself or hire a professional to interpret your ideas.

18–20 Beam detail.

18–21, 22 Getting started.

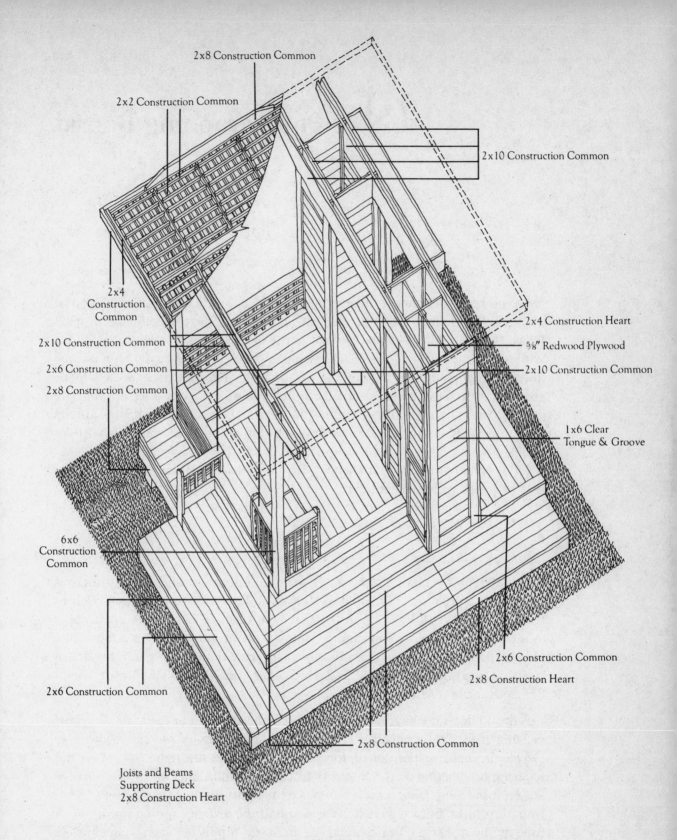

2x8 Construction Common

2x2 Construction Common

2x10 Construction Common

2x4 Construction Common

2x10 Construction Common

2x6 Construction Common

2x8 Construction Common

2x4 Construction Heart

⅝″ Redwood Plywood

2x10 Construction Common

1x6 Clear Tongue & Groove

6x6 Construction Common

2x6 Construction Common

2x6 Construction Common

2x8 Construction Heart

2x8 Construction Common

Joists and Beams Supporting Deck 2x8 Construction Heart

18-23 Basic plan. *(Photos 18-14 through 18-23 courtesy California Redwood Association (see Chapter 20, Source List))*

19. Photographing Bonsai

Even professional photographers must study a bit to produce good bonsai pictures. The trunk, roots, leaves, pot, and ground cover should be in good focus; the tree must be properly positioned; the background should be neutral with no distracting shadows. The viewing angle should not be too high nor too low but slightly above the middle of the tree. The tree is expected to be groomed at its best; the pot must be immaculate and accessories appropriate and in scale. There are rules to follow but reason, balance—even heart—are the real criteria. The significance of a fine tree can be lost if the photo is without feeling.

Indoor photos are most satisfactory, since you control all factors, and there is no wind with which to contend.

LIGHTING

Acceptable photographs can be made with an ordinary flash bulb, but there is likely to be a problem of unwanted shadows and it's unlikely that the details of trunk and roots will show up. A better way to shoot indoor photos of bonsai is to set up floodlights. A flood lamp, which costs around $15, has a bowl-like reflector that holds a special bulb more powerful than those made for house lamps. A good bulb is General Electric's E.C.A. or Sylvania's 500-watt Photo-Ect, both made for this purpose.

A flood lamp may have a clamp which can be attached to the back of a chair or other place, but a tripod is far better, making it possible to raise, lower, or swivel the light to position it for best effect. Turn the lights off when not focusing or shooting as the intensity of the heat and light can injure a tree if left on it too long. Directions say to place the lights not less than 4 feet (1.2 m) from the object, but we have had them at half the distance for ten minutes at a time without harm. Two should be used to supply a strong, shadowless illumination without washing out depth. They can be on either side and slightly to the front, with one focused down and one on a level with the trunk. Focus them on the tree and turned slightly away from the camera.

Extra light can be reflected from a glass-beaded home projector screen and|or a large white sheet of posterboard from an art supply shop. The screen will have its own stand. You can set the poster board on the other side of the bonsai, propped on a chair. Tests show that better results are obtained with flat-white reflecting surfaces rather than glossy-white surfaces, mirrors, or bright foil as the light from flat white is luminous and diffused while shinier surfaces make harsh reflections.

FILM

If you are using daylight color film (Kodachrome 64 is good), you'll need a filter—such as No. 80A—which is of blue-tinted glass and screws onto the camera lens. It will assure good, true color at a modest cost—somewhere between $7 and $9 for a 35 mm camera. For all black and white photography, the use of a skylight filter (No. 1A) is helpful in reducing the adverse effects of atmospheric haze.

Since enlargements will probably be made—8 X 10 glossies if you are submitting your photos to a publisher—a slower film is best, making a fine textured, clear portrait. Plus-X panchromatic is a medium fast black-and-white film good for indoor floods, time exposures, and a wide range of light conditions out of doors. For the perfectionist who wants the finest textured enlargements, there is Panatomic-X, a slower film which must have strong light and a tripod or very steady support for the camera. All the films mentioned are manufactured by the Kodak company, although many other fine films are available.

CAMERAS

The camera can be a simple, inexpensive one and still give pretty good pictures, but much better results are accomplished with a single-lens reflex type having a through-the-lens light meter. A standard lens, like the 50 mm f/1.2, 50 mm f/1.4, or 55 mm f/1.8 with fully automatic diaphragm, will give good sharp focusing from about one and one half feet (.45 m) to infinity. Of these, I prefer the f/1.4. It is fast enough and bright enough to give a thoroughly satisfactory picture. A camera like this has a self-timer for delayed shutter action, through-the-lens focusing (what you see is what you get!), and many other bonuses.

Most intriguing to me is the wide variety of lenses which snap or screw on and off the camera body easily. There are close-up lenses, zoom lenses galore (what a joy to be able to zoom in on tiny objects!), wide-angle lenses, telescopic lenses—even a lens that takes shots at right angles to the apparent focusing direction. For our use here, the 50 mm Macro f/4 is excellent, for it focuses from close-ups of 0.77 feet (0.234 m), through the in-between distances, to infinity, eliminating the need for a standard lens altogether. A wide-angle, like a 28 mm f/3.5, is useful for photographing a whole collection, gardens, or — since it can be focused as close as one foot (0.3 m)—it's good for a long, low shape that a regular lens wouldn't accommodate as a closeup.

With all through-the-lens light meters keep the lens cap on when not focusing or shooting because the meter is on, using battery energy, whenever the lens cap is off. It's a simple matter to snap it off for use. It protects the front element of your lens as well as the light meter.

KEEPING THE CAMERA STEADY

Since it's unlikely you'll be able to hold the camera steady enough by hand, brace it against a chair-back, your knee, table, wall, or whatever is available. Even better, borrow or buy a tripod ($20—$30 up). This is a lovely thing to have. The legs telescope from 1 foot to 4 or 5 feet, the stem holding the camera can be adjusted by several inches, and the camera is held firmly in place, to be used either level or tilted sideways for taller, more slender shapes. Remove the camera from its case if it has one. The tripod can screw into the case fitting but the camera will not be held as firmly. The tripod should have a firm surface. If its legs are resting on thick carpeting, hold the tripod by its middle stem and press down as you trip the shutter. Or you can set the tripod on a piece of plywood.

Another highly recommended refinement is the cable release. This device trips the shutter once all focusing is done without jarring the camera in the slightest.

The reason for all this caution about jarring the camera is that indoor photos are taken at a reduced shutter speed; the shutter is open longer, increasing the likelihood that a picture will be blurred because of a tiny movement that would not matter at a faster shutter speed. I find it necessary to set the shutter speed at 1/30th second, which makes a steady camera imperative.

COMPOSITION

The tree, pot, base, and accessories (if any) are treated as a unit, and enough area is left around this unit to make the objects seem comfortable, not cramped. No part of a leaf or base should touch the edge or be cut off. Conversely, if too much free space is left, the composition looks lost and of diminished importance. Also be sure the camera is square with the pot and table.

The depth of field—the space that is in exact focus—will be shorter as you move the camera closer. In focusing for depth you'll have to choose what details are most important; unless you especially desire trunk detail, for instance, you will probably want to focus midway between the trunk and the near leaves. This splits the difference, giving a fair overall focus.

BACKGROUND

Use a plain or neutral background. A blank wall is fine if it has a low gloss or matte finish. Plain drapes or very small-patterned wallpaper are good or one might buy a roll of photographer's background paper ($12 and up) which is excellent. Photographer's paper comes in many colors and rug-size rolls; it can be secured to a support or taped to a wall then brought down over the floor or table in a single sweep, making a seamless, unobtrusive background. The roll probably will be much larger than necessary for your purposes so you'll need to cut it to size.

Well-stocked art supply shops offer large, colored posterboard (figs. 19–1, 2),

19–1, 2 Outdoor photography of bonsai presents problems; the light may be too bright (too much contrast) or from the wrong direction. Your subject may blend into the trees beyond. One solution is offered here. Note the tree is placed for minimum shadow-cast. Wind is another factor. We taped these placards in place!

from 24 X 30 inches up to 40 X 60 inches. This last usually comes only in white. Cost runs from $1 to $5 each. Many interesting effects can be brought into play with posterboards; I like to use one for the floor and one for the wall. Both can be in one color or you might try a medium blue floor with a light blue wall, for example, or a black floor with a red wall, or a brown floor with a yellow wall. Use whatever best complements the tree.

You may be surprised at what a large background you need for even a small tree. Before buying the material sight through the camera at the tree, focus in, and determine how large a sheet is necessary. You don't want the edges to show!

Woven grass beach mats are another good possibility for a background, and they are long enough and flexible enough to be used as photographer's background paper.

Flood lamps can be arranged so as to eliminate shadows, even on a close background. If you are using a flash or natural light, the background ought to be farther away.

Outside, a fence, wall, or blue sky can be used. Always check for distracting details before shooting. The outdoor scenery includes such indigenous objects as a garden hose, tools, a doghouse, etc.—objects which you might overlook since they are always there, but the camera won't.

Bright, direct sun will make strong shadows and, unless you plan carefully, trunks may photograph in deep shadow (see fig. 19–2). The diffused light of an overcast sky is far better, and is surprisingly bright.

It's amazing how good it is for one's collection when photos are to be taken. The plants are cleaned and groomed and styled in a more objective way, as if one is seeing through the eyes of a stranger.

Whether the pictures are for your own files or are to be submitted to a publication, the same standards apply: well-groomed plants, sharp focus, and a balanced, uncluttered composition.

KEEPING RECORDS

It's useful if you record the date, botanical name if known, size (height from ground to tip of tree), caliper (diameter of trunk), and note down any other information that seems pertinent. If you leaf-cut only every other year, you could make a note of whether this was done in the year of the photo. Indicate if this particular tree is very late to leaf out in the spring or if it reacts poorly to certain insecticides.

All this information is tremendously useful if coupled with a yearly portrait. It helps us to learn about the tree and observe the results of our work each year. If the tree should be sold, given, or willed to another, such a biography becomes even more important.

20. Sources

The sources below are ones I am familiar with. Of course, there are many others. You might query your local garden centers, check the Yellow Pages, or consult bonsai experts in your area.

CALIFORNIA

Eastside Irrigation Service,
645 West Lamona, Fresno, 93725
Automatic watering timers. Complete kits for watering containerized plants.

Armstrong Nurseries,
Box 473, Ontario, 91764
Young starter plants. Dwarf citrus.

California Redwood Association,
617 Montgomery St.,
San Francisco, 94111.
Plans for garden shelters.

Crane Products,
8432 Birch Bark Dr.,
Pico Rovera, 90660
Handcrafted bonsai tools. Starter plants.

Montebello Nursery,
1325 Fremont

Los Altos 94022
Bonsai and young pre-bonsai.

Hortica Gardens,
Don and Pauline Croxton, Box 308,
Placerville, 95667
Bonsai stock (extensive selection).
Phone (916) 622-7089

FLORIDA

House of Bonsai,
800 Trail Blvd., No.,
Naples, 33940
Mature bonsai. Young starter stock. Pots and accessories.
Phone (813) 597-4308

Pottingers' Nursery,
P.O. Box 574,
900 Sunset Vista Dr.,
Ft. Myers, 33902
Wholesale and Retail.

Young starter stock. Good selection of larger shrubs and palms.

HAWAII

Fuku Bonsai nursery,
Box 178, Kurtistown, 96760
Bonsai planted on lava rock, bonsai tropicals.

MISSOURI

Southwood Nursery,
8553 Everett Ave.,
St. Louis, 63117
*Bonsai courses by Joel Gold.
Pots, tools, indoor and outdoor bonsai. Small starter stock.*
Phone (314) 721-3392

Sunset Plantland,
3850 So. Lindberg,
St. Louis, 63127
*Pots and live material.
Good selection indoor plants and small pines.*
Phone (314) 843-7445

OHIO

Keith Scott,
17771 Snyder Rd.,
Chagrin Falls, 44022
Pots. Young starter stock.

Gierard Nurseries,
P.O. Box 428,
Geneva, 44041
Starter bonsai: fine selection of species
rhododendrons, miniature type spruce, other stock especially suitable for bonsai.

Mellingers' Inc.,
2310 W. South Range,
North Lima, 44452
Extensive selection small trees and shrubs.

OREGON

Greer Gardens,
1280 Goodpasture Island Rd.,
Eugene, 97401
Very large selection starter plants. Fine variety species rhododendron and Japanese maples.

TEXAS

The Bonsai Farm, R.1 Box 156,
Adkins, 78101
Good variety plants for indoor and outdoor bonsai. Tools, and pots.

ENGLAND

Hillier Nurseries (Winchester) LTD,*
20/26 Lamb's Conduit Street,
London WCIN 3LE
This one is included because of its very complete and very worthwhile catalogue, which is an education in itself. Write for catalogue price, including self-addressed envelope, with full postage, not in U.S. stamps, but in international postage certificates available at your post office.

Index

acer, 110
Acer buergerianum, 11, 53
Acer ginella, 17
accent plants, 50, 64, 80
acoris, 57, 64
acrylics, 49
air layering, 28, 30
aldrin, 171
algae, 154
ants, 152, 171, 172
arenarea, 62, 65
artificial moss, 23
ash, 84
auxin, 40
azalea, 64, 79, 81, 85, 160, 166, 171

beech, 38, 53, 84, 87, 151
Benemyl, 165, 169
betula, 87
birch, 82, 87, 162, 173
bite cutters, 140
black leaf-spot, 170
bone meal, 77
bonsai fertilizer, 23
Bordeaux, 171
botrytis, 169
box, 38, 57, 82, 88, 162
branches, 2, 3, 6, 38
bromeliad, 68
broom style, 6, 44
buxus, 17, 82, 88

calcium, 166
camellias, 162

carissa, 115, 162
cascade (style), 6, 41
Catlin elm, 160, 162
celtis, 102
chamaecyparis, 79, 81, 104, 162
chaenomeles, 120
chewing insects, 172
Chinese elm, 92 (see: Ulmus, elm)
chlordane, 171, 173
chrysanthemums, 160, 162
Chumono, 3
cloud or umbrella (style), 9
compost, 77, 131
copper, 166
copper wire, 35, 58, 144
cotoneaster, 82, 90
crape myrtle, 90, 160
crataegus, 103
cryptomeria, 79, 81, 106, 162
cuttings, 30
cutworms, 174
cyperus, 71

dandelion, 70
deciduous trees, 32, 35, 45, 46, 79, 81, 158
Diazinon, 172, 174
Dieldrin, 171
diseases, 150, 165
dormant oils, 171
dwarf baby tears (see: Helxine soleirolii), 70
dwarf Egyptian papyrus, 71
dwarf horsetail (Equisetum), 71